HOW TO PROFIT FROM
FORMULA PLANS
IN THE STOCK MARKET

FORTUNE BUILDING LIBRARY

HOW TO PROFIT FROM
FORMULA PLANS
IN THE STOCK MARKET

BY
DAVID JENKINS

AMERICAN RESEARCH COUNCIL
LARCHMONT, NEW YORK

CONTENTS

TABLES and CHARTS

Tables

Charts

HOW YOU CAN PUT FORMULAS
TO PROFITABLE USE

A famous Wall Street story concerns a young man who was in the early stages of learning to be a professional speculator. He had a problem, so he went for advice to an elderly sage noted for his shrewd investment judgment. The fact was, the young man said, that he had taken on quite an extensive line of stocks, but the market looked high—maybe too high—he thought possibly his position carried with it too many risks, and wondered if he shouldn't perhaps sell. He was so worried about this, he said, that he couldn't sleep nights.

The old man's counsel was simple and direct: "Sell," he said. "Sell back to the sleeping point."

Although there is no doubt that this advice smacks of imprecision, there is a good bit of wisdom in it. We may fairly assume that neither the young man nor his adviser knew for sure which way the market was going, but both were aware that the market was sufficiently shaky to cause legitimate worry. Translated into somewhat more orthodox investment terms, the advice meant: "Sell enough of your stocks so that a market collapse won't destroy you, but keep enough so that if your fears turn out to be groundless, and the market rises, you'll still profit to some extent; in the meantime, get some sleep."

At first glance, it may seem cynical on the old man's part not to outline for his protege an exact and detailed course of action. But he could not honestly guarantee that he knew exactly what action might turn out to be best. Furthermore, the young man didn't want someone to tell him precisely what to do. All

9

he wanted was some help in easing the pressure at a critical point, and the help he got seems eminently sensible.

FINDING THE "SLEEPING POINT"

In a real sense, the investment formulas described in this book are designed to help you in the same way that the old man's advice helped his young friend—they inject an element of caution in your investing when caution seems advisable, they reduce the provision for caution when risks seem relatively low, and permit you to benefit from rising prices for common stocks. Moreover, once you incorporate a formula into your investment program, it works more or less automatically, thus allowing you to sleep nights in the knowledge that you are continuously hedging against various possibilities.

But just as the investment sage left it up to the young man to decide exactly what the "sleeping point" might be in his particular case, you can select a formula appropriate to your own temperament, financial circumstances and proclivity to insomnia. As will be made clear in later pages of this book, any of the formulas can be adjusted to suit the needs and preferences of any investor.

Although formulas are designed to give unhedged and unambiguous indications for action, the investor should not feel that he is therefore giving up all personal control over his investments when he adopts a formula, since he selects it himself to fit his own requirements. A formula does not try to tell you what to do—it merely helps you do what you are already doing more profitably. For example, formulas cannot tell you which stocks to buy. This book assumes that anyone interested in formulas is already a relatively sophisticated investor and knows what kind of stocks he wants to buy, how to select them and where to go for advice in his particular areas of interest. But— by supplementing his knowledge of *which* securities with considerations of the equally important questions of *when* to own them and *in what quantity*—formulas can supply a valuable added dimension to his investment results and help put the management of his portfolio on a more professional level.

Along this same line, it is worth mentioning that although

the true purpose of a formula is to supply the investor with an investment policy which is definite in its instructions at all times, you need not feel that you must follow the formula precisely in order to profit from it. You cannot, of course, ignore it altogether if you expect to benefit from it, but you can profitably use it as a touchstone or a general guide without swearing eternal allegiance to its dictates. You might, for example, want to use a formula, but also desire to increase or decrease your risks at various times for some reason. Your use of the formula will show you how far you are departing from your original plan, and will give you a well-ordered program to come back to when you are ready.

WHAT A FORMULA DOES

What, exactly, does a formula do? This question will be answered in considerable detail in later sections of this book, but a summary of a formula's usefulness would include two main functions it fulfills.

First, over a full stock market cycle, it will improve your investment profits without the application of any thought whatever on your part. As is well known, there are many investors who do not believe that the market will ever go through a full cycle again—that the direction of the market is in a permanently upward movement, except for temporary, minor dips. It might be worthwhile to point out—without seeming to be pessimistic —that there are some good arguments against an indefinite continuation of bull markets.

In the 12-year period from June, 1949, to June, 1961, the market—as measured by the Dow-Jones Industrial Average— rose over 300 percent, a compound rate of gain of about 13 percent annually. Assuming that there is some connection between the nation's economy and the stock market, this rate of gain in the market cannot be maintained indefinitely, because the economy ordinarily grows at a rate of three percent or so (this varies, but it never reaches 13 percent). Even granted that the market was too low in 1949 (which it most certainly was), that does not mean that a steady 13 percent rate of gain will not have put it too high at some point. If this perhaps gloomy suggestion turns out to be wrong, and the market does continue forever upward, then formulas will be useless, since they do assume that the stock market is quite cyclical.

The second purpose of a formula—apart from the question of profiting from *complete* market cycles—is to provide a means of profiting from more minor fluctuations. It is undeniable that the market will continue to fluctuate, and a formula allows the investor to benefit from these fluctuations by specifying conservative investment policies when the market is relatively high, and more aggressive policies when it is relatively low.

Since formulas ordinarily appear rather complicated, can the small investor profitably use them? The answer is definitely *yes*. Some formulas are complicated, it is true, and the reader will find in later pages some that are so complex as to be unsuitable for most investors. But most formulas do not fall into this category. The most widely used formulas today, in fact, are based on extremely simple principles and can be used by anyone with a rough knowledge of grade-school arithmetic. Special measures to adapt formulas to the needs of small investors will be discussed to some extent later on, but it is worth noting that small investors are just as likely to want to improve their profit performance in the market as are larger investors. And there is no particular disadvantage in having a small portfolio when you use a formula.

SECURITY vs. UNCERTAINTY

All investors—large, small and medium-size—are in the same basic quandary. They would like to be sure of what is going to happen to their capital, and so are inclined to appreciate the features of fixed-income investments such as savings accounts, bonds and commercial paper.

In such investments, their capital is guaranteed, and (except in the case of savings accounts) so is their interest. On the other hand, there are few opportunities for appreciable profits in these areas, and no protection against a decline in the value of the dollar. Consequently, they are attracted by the characteristics of common stocks, where neither their capital nor their return is guaranteed, but which offer substantial opportunities for profits through capital gain.

How to resolve the dilemma? It is obvious that the great difficulty with the stock market is its uncertainty. One workable suggestion of reducing the damage this uncertainty can do has been often made: don't buy common stocks at all. Most investors tend to regard this idea as, although practical, rather extreme, and are reluctant to abandon the possibilities of profit that exist in common stocks. The formula idea is simply a form of protection against uncertainty. Formulas are designed to allow the investor to profit from the advantages of owning common stocks, while providing him with a measure of protection against their handicaps; to give him some of the stability offered by fixed income investments, while not condemning him to a low return on his money. The whole point of formulas is to make the best of both these worlds.

ONE

WHAT IS A FORMULA?

The difficulties of building a fortune in the stock market are a painfully familiar subject to the large majority of those who have tried it. The gap between the apparent ease of beating the market and actual results of investors—both professional and amateur—is the principal justification for investment formulas and, hence, for this book.

A pungent argument in favor of formulas can be seen in an article in *Fortune* a few years ago.[1] Entitled "Wall Streeters Who Were Right," the essay lauds a number of financial analysts who correctly called the turn prior to the slump that began in the summer of 1957. In a piece ostensibly dedicated to the brilliance of certain forecasters, the author may have had his tongue at least partly in cheek when he blandly observed that, "significantly," the analysts in question differed in "predicting what now lies ahead." Significantly? A cynical observer might assume the significance to be that the article was not more accurately entitled "Wall Streeters Who Were Lucky," and that some of them were shortly going to cease being lucky. Obviously, if the forecasters disagreed about the market's immediate prospects, some of them were going to have to be wrong, since the market can go in only one direction at a time.

The purpose of this is not to disparage a group of men making an honest living in a notoriously difficult field, but simply to note the dangers of making dogmatic judgments on the future of stock prices. Probably the safest prediction ever made of the stock market was the succinct prophecy: "It will fluctuate," which, according to Wall Street folklore, was made by J. P. Morgan after a lengthy conference with his most trusted associates. While the story may be apocryphal, the validity of the statement is not. And the idea of formulas was developed to cope with these fluctuations and indeed to rely to some extent on their occurrence for successful investing.

FORMULAS WORK AUTOMATICALLY

An investment formula is, in essence, a device which, taking its cues from developments outside the individual investor's field of judgment, caprice or personal opinion, dictates a definite investment policy at all times. It does not select stocks, but it does indicate whether a particular time is favorable for owning stocks, and if so, in what quantities, and how much of an investor's capital should be reserved for later stock purchases at more favorable levels. And because the investor himself selects his own formula and builds into it a degree of risk consonant with his investment objectives and willingness to take risks, the instructions of the formula are always in line with the investor's own goals.

A formula's primary purpose is to provide a degree of protection against losses caused by unforeseen market swings, and in fact use these swings as an integral part of their operation, by dictating sales of stock (or reduced purchases) as the market nears a top, and increased purchases when it bounces along a low point.

Many investors, when told the market is "too high," might well want to ask: "Too high for what?" The formula tells them —and defines investment action (or lack of it) in terms of their own portfolios and investment objectives. In addition, it has— as we shall see—built-in safeguards against the indecision that tends to afflict almost every investor at some time, the temptation to become over-reckless or over-conservative, and even the imperfections of the formula itself.

The primary objective of a formula is to place the investor in a *permanent and continuous profit position*. It is gauged to produce profits—over a period of time—whatever happens in the market. When stock prices rise, his portfolio shows a profit. When they fall, he steps up his purchases at bargain levels. At intermediate points, he relies on the indications given by the formula to continuously strengthen his profit position. One of the earliest investigators in the field of formula investing drew an

15

analogy with a "thermostatic control" [2] which—like any other thermostatic control—works automatically at all times without asking the investor to use his own judgment.

From this description, it may seem that formulas are nothing but an elaborate extension of the time-honored advice to "buy low and sell high." This is, in fact, the case. The special feature of the formula method is that it tells the investor exactly what to do at all times without attempting a precise prediction of market prices. Implicit in the formula idea is that it is not possible to pinpoint every turn in the market or to gain maximum profits during every market swing. Formulas make no attempt to do this, but are aimed at putting the investor in a position to profit to *some* extent from any market upswing, and to provide *some* protection during every decline.

GROWTH OF FORMULAS

The search for automatic investing techniques—schemes which would produce profits by giving investors advance indication of market swings, based on a mechanical interpretation of market data—has been going on for quite some time. One of the earliest methods was the "Dow Theory," a set of rules for interpreting market action drawn up by William Peter Hamilton about 40 years ago, which were roughly based on the writings of Charles H. Dow. The question of how to apply the various Dow Theory rules is still subject to considerable dispute among adherents of the method, and the battle of reliability is still being bitterly contested by its supporters and detractors.

The search for mechanical market techniques accelerated after the 1929 crash, which had revealed not only the treacheries of emotion but also the frequently appalling inadequacy of even the most reputable investment advisers. The well-known debacle of the closed-end investment companies during the period following the crash—including those managed by some of the best-known names in Wall Street—indicated to many observers the near-impossibility of reliably predicting the course of stock prices. A striking result of this sad situation—and perhaps the quaintest automatic investing technique ever invented—turned up in this field. This was the so-called "fixed trust." The idea was for the trust to include in its portfolio only securities of what were universally regarded as the "best" corporations. Once set up, the portfolio was to be fully protected from the dangers of investment management. It was not to be altered in any way or for any reason . . . except one. If any corporation stopped paying dividends, its stock was to be forthwith sold. Naturally, by the time a company passes its dividend, the price of the stock usually reflects the fact that it has been in hot water for some time, so this neat gimmick did nothing but insure that stocks would be sold at true distress prices, with the inevitable deterioration of the trust's asset values. Fixed trusts are no longer an important part of the American investment scene.

Stock market forecasters did not stop forecasting during this period, but their results were far from outstanding. A famous study by Alfred Cowles, covering the period from 1928 through 1943 and including 6,904 forecasts of the market as a whole made by 11 experts, showed a score, on average, of about two-tenths of one percent better than random guesswork.[3]

Investors did not stop losing money, either. Results of an exhaustive research project conducted by Paul Francis Wendt covering the period 1933-38 (on balance, an upward period for the market), indicated that only 21.8 percent of a sample of typical customers came out with a profit.[4]

Beginning in the thirties, large numbers of automatic investing techniques were developed, bringing into existence dozens of charts, tables, trend lines, moving averages, breadth and depth indicators, complicated mathematical computations, economic indexes, banking data curves, adaptations from the recondite areas of physics and chemistry, and plenty of others. By now, it seems that every available set of statistical data has been put to some use as a forecaster of stock market trends, no matter how tenuous the connection. There is at least one investment adviser known to the writer who predicts the mysterious movements of stock averages by following the no less mysterious movements of celestial bodies.

Some of these "timing devices" are intended to work automatically, and others are subject to considerable interpretation. Some are only sporadically successful, others are worthless, and a great many of them tend to be quite complicated. The principal difficulty with such methods is that they make no allowance for errors. As we have seen, one of the characteristics of formulas is that they do not aim for one hundred percent accuracy, and always make allowances for the probable, while hedging against the possible. A formula method can, however, be combined with a timing device, and an example of this approach is given later in this book.

Eventually, the idea of an automatic formula—which would not be designed to predict market swings with any accuracy, but would still dictate a reliable investment policy, prevent large losses and produce a steady profit over any market cycle—became increasingly attractive.

Originators of formula plans, therefore, eschewed "forecasting" as far as possible, and based their policies on the single assumption that the market would continue to fluctuate—in some cases specifying approximate limits, but without trying to predict their timing.

These earliest formulas, in the late thirties and early forties, were largely the handiwork of various institutions, primarily college endowment funds. An automatic formula was especially attractive to such investors. The investment committees, often composed of non-professionals and given to policy disputes, were more than anxious to rely on a formula which would allow them to agree on investment principles and also take them off the hook in case the institution's investments didn't fare too well. One of the foremost pioneers in the field of formulas, Robert Warren (formerly director of exploratory research for Keystone Custodian Funds, Inc.) first became interested in the subject when a Keystone mutual fund distributor in Philadelphia called for help in the case of a local hospital's finance committee which couldn't decide on an investment policy for the hospital's endowed funds. Warren drew up a formula, which presumably satisfied the committee, and went on to explore formulas extensively in subsequent years.

Although the original impetus for formulas came from such large institutions, many of them have long since discarded the formula idea. On the other hand, a rising trend of popularity has been seen in the use of formulas by individuals, perhaps as a result of market experience in recent years, which has so often and so regrettably proved the experts wrong. A number of investment counselors, in fact, have adopted the policy of selling their services on the basis of formula investing techniques.[5]

DO FORMULAS WORK?

The fact that some formulas have wound up in the junk heap after they proved inadequate to changed market conditions has led same observers to conclude that the whole idea must have been poor from the start. This is like saying that because the great majority of automobile companies have folded over the years, the automobile must therefore be a failure.

Many of the earlier formulas were, in fact, poorly devised, resting on inflexible, illogical and fallacious assumptions. Even some of these, however, performed their function well for some time. Many of the basic faults that afflicted the earlier methods have been recognized, and present-day techniques are considerably improved. The reasons behind the early fallacies will be explored more fully in other sections of this book, but it should be pointed out that they did have the virtue of pointing the way toward better use of the formula idea.

In answering the inquiry of whether formulas "work"—certainly a fair question on the part of an investor who may want to subject a large part of his funds to a formula's dictates—we must first ask what we mean by saying that *any* investment technique "works."

The de Vegh Mutual Fund, Inc., has answered this question —for itself—by stipulating that the fund's management fee is to be chopped in half in any year that the fund's asset-value performance fails to beat the Dow-Jones Industrial Average by two percentage points, which seems a wholly admirable and unequivocal method of defining the intentions of the fund. In this case, management's methods have "worked," and it has earned its full fee in most years since the fund was founded in 1950.

Admittedly, designation of the Dow-Jones Industrials is a somewhat arbitrary choice. Why not the Rails, or the Utilities, or the 65-Stock Composite Average? There is no reason why some other average could not be chosen with equal logic. The point is that the fund states its objective in no uncertain terms, which doesn't necessarily mean that some other way of setting an objective would not be equally valid.

19

To take a different example, an amateur trader who has suffered sizable losses in aimless speculation might feel that any technique that promises to yield more than the neighborhood savings bank is one that "works." For many unsuccessful and embittered speculators, in fact, any method that simply preserved their capital intact would represent a gain over their instinctive systems of "playing the market."

Some studies have shown that, theoretically, profits are by no means difficult to come by in the stock market. A well-known investment principle which first gained wide popularity in Edgar Lawrence Smith's "Common Stocks as Long-Term Investments" (1924) is based on the premise that satisfactory profits may be obtained simply by buying blue-chip commons and hanging on to them for a period of years.

This technique, frequently known as the "buy and hold" method of investing, has a rather large following. The basic principle behind the theory is that the long-term trend of the U.S. economy is upward, and that common stock prices will in general reflect this upward trend over the long term. A "buy and hold" investor who began operations at any time in the 1949-60 period would have had rather acceptable results even over the relatively short term.

But most active investors either do not accept the "buy and hold" theory, are dissatisfied with the inactivity it forces on them, or would prefer to shoot for profits over a shorter period of time than the "buy and hold" theory permits. And a great many investors lose money. Why?

THE ANSWER TO LOSSES

The answer undoubtedly lies in two areas—poor advice and erratic, emotional behavior. Poor advice can come from friends, brokers and advisory services who happen to be wrong. Obviously, it is impossible to detect just how poor the advice is until it is too late, and guarding against it is virtually impossible, especially for the neophyte investor.

Emotionalism is another matter. Carefully controlled classroom experiments in speculative behavior have shown that, even when relieved of paying commissions on numerous transactions and of the emotional involvement of handling real money, people tend to chalk up heavier losses than gains—very much as they do in actual investing.[6] Furthermore, the lack of correlation between speculative success and (1) intelligence or (2) professional investment experience, suggests that some set of as-yet-unknown emotional factor is at work.

Donald I. Rogers, Business and Financial Editor of the New York *Herald Tribune*, quoted an unnamed broker to the effect that many investors lose money intentionally (on an unconscious level) in order to assuage deep feelings of guilt.[7] Whether or not this is so, the fact is that few investors are really successful in the market. They tend to buy a stock on the crest of its rise, hold it while it goes down, and sell in disgust either before it recovers or when it rises barely enough to produce a slim profit.

There is no reliable method of finding out how successful individual investors are today. But if the Wendt study of investor experience in the thirties is any indication, we may assume that many of them have little reason to be satisfied with their results.

For those investors whose results are somewhat less than brilliant, formulas can supply an answer, and probably can be said to "work," by any reasonable standard. They most certainly help to protect the investor against the dangers of emotionalism, and offer a guide to action that can protect him from acting under the perhaps unwise impulse of the moment. Furthermore, they do not freeze him in an inflexible vise that prevents him from exercising his own judgment or irritates him through lack of action, but they do supply a measure of self-discipline. And if the formula is adhered to with some degree of tenacity, the investor's results should be improved to a great extent.

While it is probably an exaggeration to assert that "any plan is better than no plan," even a mediocre plan may produce better results than those attained by the average hit-or-miss investor, alternately subject to panic, agonies of indecision, impulsive action on ill-advised tips and a hundred other damaging influences.

The essential element for success in the use of a formula is consistent and unwavering application of its rules of operation. Once an investor selects a plan, he can expect satisfactory results only if he sticks reasonably close to it, no matter how bleak the short-term outlook may be. As will be seen, the route to an impressive record of profitable performance is littered with brief periods of relatively unfavorable action. But the simplicity of formulas, and their clear-cut indications for action, make them much more practical even under such adverse circumstances than most other investment techniques.

In short, *formulas will not endow the investor with brains if he doesn't already have them, but they do reduce the quantity of brains necessary to come out of the market with a profit.*

Inasmuch as a number of formulas are discussed in this book, it might logically be expected that one could be singled out as the champion profit-producer. Unfortunately, this cannot be the case. It will be obvious to the reader, of course, that some of the formulas discussed are better than others. Among those which are sound, simple, practical and profitable, however, there is no way of predicting in advance which might prove most satisfactory for any particular investor over any particular period of time.

In the first place, where one formula might gain a slight edge over another in a declining market, another might prove out slightly better in a period of rising stock prices. A comparison of two such disparate methods during any one period, therefore, does not prove very much.

Second, formulas vary in their suitability for a particular individual's circumstances. Some are ideally suited to the investor who has little capital to start with, but expects to have a continuing flow of income which he intends to devote to stock purchases. Others can be adapted to such circumstances with difficulty if at all. Only the investor can choose which method suits his needs best.

Third, some formulas require some record-keeping and a fair amount of calculation, while others call for almost none.

OTHER FACTORS

The investor who enjoys—or at least doesn't mind—occupying himself with such things would find these formulas well adapted to his talents, while one who does not wish to bother with any more than a minimum of detail would be foolish to begin managing his investments by one of these plans, because he almost certainly would abandon it within a short time. And if a plan is not followed, can it truly be said to be useful? In the same vein, the suggestion is made at several points in this book that the investor who has a sizable sum of money to invest should invest it slowly over a period of years. Understandably, some investors do not care for this approach, in which case this suggestion is of no value.

Too, there is simply the matter of personal taste. One investor might find a certain formula to fit his own ideas of investing perfectly, either for what he feels to be good and logical reasons or simply because it feels best. This writer attempts to give impartially the arguments for and against all the formulas discussed. Where the arguments for or against a particular approach appear overwhelming, this point is made, but it is not the intention to make up the reader's mind for him. After all, there are no universally accepted opinions in investing; if there were, all investors would want to buy and sell the same securities at the same time, and markets would be impossible.

Finally, none of the formulas in this book are meant to be adopted in quite the same way by any two investors. All can be modified and adjusted by the investor himself. All the necessary tools are given to allow you to make whatever alterations you feel are necessary.

From the earliest research in formula investing, authorities on the subject have emphasized that "the idea of a ready-made plan, which investors are supposed to follow exactly, is not the proper approach to the problem." [8] Every investor has different tastes, needs, prejudices and objectives, and therefore should have a formula which is adapted to them. Lucile Tomlinson, who probably knows more about formulas than anyone else, in referring to her experience in helping investors to draw up formulas, states, "As far as I can recall, no two completed plans have been exactly the same in all details." [9]

No one who has studied the subject of formulas would pretend that any is perfect. The very theory of a formula, in fact, includes the assumption that it will always be *somewhat* wrong, but that it will also always be somewhat right, and that it will be more right than wrong over a period of time.

TWO

INVESTMENT "MAGIC": DOLLAR AVERAGING

In a story in early 1959 on a decision by the State of New Mexico to invest 25 percent of its $159 million Permanent Fund in common stocks (as against a previous practice of holding the entire fund in high grade bonds), it was reported that the $59 million bundle would be sunk into equities under a "slow, four-and-a-half year program," calling for stock purchases of about $1.1 million a month.[1]

This application of what has come to be known as *dollar averaging* (or dollar cost averaging) is striking evidence of the high prestige of this investment formula. Although dollar averaging is usually thought of in connection with the small investor, a large number of institutions have long been practitioners—especially those such as pension funds, which deal with a constant flow of incoming cash.

The New Mexico example is significant in that it involves a sum of money already on hand. A look at the special circumstances shows why the New Mexico Investment Council, responsible for investing the money, picked the dollar averaging approach. A majority of the eight council members were described as "amateurs" in investing and were undoubtedly reluctant to take the blame for making a quick, big plunge in the market at what might turn out to be the wrong moment—especially in view of the all-time high level of stock prices at the time. As it happened, the market did rise considerably for some time after the initial decision was made. It is therefore easy to say that the plan was wrong, since some stocks could have been bought at lower prices if a sizable portion of the money had been invested right at the start. However, it must not be forgotten that quite a large amount of money was involved, and even an investment professional would not be eager to take the responsibility for deciding that any particular moment might be the appropriate time to invest $159 million. Then too, the council members were in positions of public responsibility, and were thus doubly on the spot.

PRINCIPLE OF DOLLAR AVERAGING

The idea of dollar averaging is to purchase the same dollar amount of a stock or stocks at regular intervals—monthly, quarterly or annually. Naturally, the method is especially appealing to small investors, who perhaps would not be able to buy stocks any other way, and it has been publicized primarily by the New York Stock Exchange in connection with its Monthly Investment Plan, and by mutual fund marketing organizations.

Buying stock at regular intervals seems a completely practical and relatively painless way of accumulating a sizable account. More important, however, the automatic result of buying a fixed dollar amount of stocks at each purchase point—instead of, say, a fixed number of shares—is that *more shares are bought at low points, and fewer at high points.* By increasing the number of shares purchased when prices are low, and cutting down as prices rise, the investor is constantly working to reduce his average cost, so that the average cost of shares purchased is always lower than the average of the prices paid.

For a clearer picture of exactly what this means, take a look at Table 1, showing results of a hypothetical dollar averaging program using the stock of Bond Stores. Over the 15-year period beginning in 1944, the stock rose sharply from the twenties to a high of nearly 50 in 1946, dropped slowly in succeeding years, and recovered near the end of the period. Our dollar averaging program assumes purchases of $1,000 worth of stock on the last trading day of each year, at an approximate average of the high and low prices of that day, the last purchase being made in 1958. The first purchase is at 22¼, and the last at 21⅛, with purchases in intervening years ranging from a high of 39½ to a low of 13⅛. Thus we see the operation of the plan over a complete market cycle, in which stock is bought above as well as below

25

the initial price, and the last purchase is near the same price as the first. Neither commissions nor dividends are included in the calculations, and investment of the $1,000 in full and fractional shares is assumed.

TABLE 1

BOND STORES
Dollar Averaging Program, 1944-58

YEAR	AMOUNT INVESTED	PRICE	NO. SHARES PURCHASED	TOTAL NO. SHARES PURCHASED	TOTAL AMOUNT INVESTED	TOTAL MKT. VALUE	AVG. OF PRICES PAID	AVG. COST PER SHARE
1944	$1,000	22¼ *	44.85	44.85	$1,000	$1,000.00	22.25	22.25
1945	1,000	39½	25.32	70.17	2,000	2,771.72	30.88	28.50
1946	1,000	31½	31.74	101.91	3,000	3,210.17	31.08	29.54
1947	1,000	25½	39.22	141.13	4,000	3,598.82	29.69	28.34
1948	1,000	17	58.82	199.95	5,000	3,399.25	27.15	25.01
1949	1,000	15⅜	65.04	264.99	6,000	4,073.22	25.19	22.64
1950	1,000	16¾	59.64	324.63	7,000	5,457.55	23.98	21.56
1951	1,000	14	71.43	396.06	8,000	5,544.84	22.93	20.20
1952	1,000	14	71.43	467.49	9,000	6,544.86	21.76	19.25
1953	1,000	13⅛	76.19	543.68	10,000	7,125.80	20.90	18.39
1954	1,000	17½	57.14	600.82	11,000	10,514.25	20.59	18.31
1955	1,000	16¾	59.65	660.47	12,000	10,462.87	20.27	18.17
1956	1,000	14⅜	69.57	730.04	13,000	10,494.33	19.77	17.81
1957	1,000	14½	68.97	799.01	14,000	11,585.64	19.64	17.52
1958	1,000	21⅛	47.33	846.34	15,000	17,878.93	19.55	17.61

*Adjusted for 2-for-1 split in 1945.

The number of shares purchased ranges from 31.74 in 1946, to 76.19 in 1953. Over the 15-year period, a total of $15,000 is invested, and total market value is $17,878.93 at the end of the plan. While this may seem an unexciting result, it should be noted that the stock itself has not only made no progress at all, but has lost ground.

The reason for the satisfactory result despite relatively poor market performance is, as stated above, that at any time after the beginning of the plan, the average cost of shares purchased is lower than the average of prices paid, because fewer shares are bought at high prices, more at low prices. The discrepancy between the average of prices paid and average cost per share is shown in the table. Not shown in the table are dividends, which would have been considerable, amounting to about $1,000 during the last year alone. The main point, however, is that our hypothetical investor did much better by buying his stock in slow stages than he would have done by purchasing $15,000 worth at the beginning.

A LONG-TERM PROFIT PROFILE

Results of another hypothetical experiment, this one based on the market as a whole, are presented in a booklet published by the New York Stock Exchange.[2] The booklet reports the conclusions of a study made by two professors at the Bureau of Business Research at the University of Michigan, designed to test the effectiveness of dollar averaging over a complete market cycle. The period began January 15, 1937, and ended January 15, 1950. This period had the advantage of being long enough to give a fair picture, and the market—as measured by the Dow-Jones Industrials—stood at approximately the same point at the end as at the beginning. To eliminate the danger of hindsight, the researchers used a total of 92 stocks, selected by a mechanical method, but, as it turned out, representing a broad cross-section of American industry.

It was assumed that $1,000 worth of each stock was bought on January 15—an arbitrarily selected date—of each year during the period. In addition, all dividends paid during the preceding year on the shares already held were assumed to be added to the $1,000 and invested at the same time. On this basis, a total of $1,288,000 was theoretically invested, plus $850,182 in dividends. At the end of the period, total value of the account was $3,028,855 (commissions were not considered).

An interesting twist was added by the professors when they rearranged the stocks in other random groupings consisting of fewer stocks, with essentially the same results. They then picked 27 of the best-performing stocks and ran the same test on them —here, $378,000 invested, plus reinvested dividends grew to $1,073,841. The same amount put into 27 of the worst performers grew to $693,424—less startling, but still an adequate profit.

In both these hypothetical cases it was assumed that prices ended up in very much the same spot where they started. What happens if prices are not quite so accommodating? If the stock or stocks selected by the dollar-averager turn sour, and never recover to the starting point, is it still possible to salvage any of the investment?

Reference was made in the introduction to the oft-voiced theory that "any plan is better than no plan." In dollar averaging, this may be literally true, and the hypothetical case history presented in Table 2 is a good demonstration of this.

BUILDING A FORTUNE WITH A "LEMON"

It would be difficult to find a stock which was so highly regarded prior to the 1929 crash and at the same time so totally lacking in true investment merit as Radio Corporation of America. Manipulated by a highly skilled and superbly organized pool operation, the stock, which had never paid a dividend, was pushed to a mid-1929 high of over 500. A steady barrage of publicity kept the public in a state of high excitement about the company's supposedly rosy future in the new wonderland of radio. Eventually, the stock's fans were doomed to disappointment. It eventually lost over 95 percent of its market value as measured from the high point, and to this day has not recovered to its 1929 peak. Still, the stock was highly respected at the time, and an investor could hardly be blamed for picking Radio as the stock most likely to succeed in future years, or for building a dollar averaging program around it.

Table 2 assumes that $1,000 was invested in the stock at an average of the high and low prices of the last trading day of each year, beginning in 1928, and continuing until 1960, making a total investment of $33,000. (Commissions are disregarded, and it is assumed that all the $1,000 was invested in full and fractional shares.)

As the table shows, the initial purchase was made at 75⅛ in 1928 (adjusted for a 5-for-1 split in 1929), when 13.31 shares were bought. At the low point in 1941, the stock was selling at 2½, and 400 shares were purchased. By 1931 the stock had already lost most of its value, and the dollar averager scored a loss, but not in proportion to the stock's decline. The table takes for granted that our intrepid investor finds it possible to raise the necessary cash in each year during the depression, and that he sinks it into his pet stock. His investment doesn't move solidly into the profit column until 1943. After that date, of course, the steady purchases at low prices in the thirties begin to pay off, and a small rise is sufficient to produce a fat profit. At the

TABLE 2

RADIO CORPORATION OF AMERICA
Dollar Averaging Program, 1928-58

YEAR	AMOUNT INVESTED	PRICE	NO. SHARES PURCHASED	TOTAL NO. SHARES PURCHASED	TOTAL COST	TOTAL MARKET VALUE
1928	$1,000	75⅛ *	13.31	13.31	$1,000	1,000.00
1929	1,000	43¼	23.12	36.43	2,000	1,575.66
1930	1,000	12⅛	82.47	118.90	3,000	1,441.71
1931	1,000	5⅝	177.78	296.68	4,000	1,668.81
1932	1,000	5¼	190.48	487.16	5,000	2,557.57
1933	1,000	6¾	148.15	635.31	6,000	4,288.44
1934	1,000	5½	181.81	817.12	7,000	4,494.16
1935	1,000	12⅜	80.89	898.01	8,000	11,112.87
1936	1,000	11½	86.96	984.97	9,000	11,327.16
1937	1,000	6	166.67	1,151.64	10,000	6,909.84
1938	1,000	7⅞	127.02	1,278.66	11,000	10,069.53
1939	1,000	5½	181.81	1,460.47	12,000	8,032.64
1940	1,000	4⅝	214.05	1,674.52	13,000	7,744.70
1941	1,000	2½	400.00	2,074.52	14,000	5,186.32
1942	1,000	5	200.00	2,274.52	15,000	11,372.65
1943	1,000	9½	105.26	2,379.78	16,000	22,608.00
1944	1,000	10½	95.24	2,475.02	17,000	25,987.81
1945	1,000	17⅜	57.55	2,532.57	18,000	44,003.57
1946	1,000	9¼	108.11	2,640.68	19,000	24,426.38
1947	1,000	9⅜	106.45	2,747.13	20,000	25,754.43
1948	1,000	13⅝	73.39	2,820.52	21,000	38,429.72
1949	1,000	12½	80.00	2,900.52	22,000	36,256.63
1950	1,000	16½	60.61	2,961.13	23,000	48,858.81
1951	1,000	23⅝	41.91	3,003.04	24,000	70,947.06
1952	1,000	28½	35.09	3,038.13	25,000	86,586.99
1953	1,000	23⅛	43.24	3,081.37	26,000	71,256.68
1954	1,000	38¾	25.81	3,107.18	27,000	120,403.33
1955	1,000	47	21.28	3,128.46	28,000	147,037.62
1956	1,000	35⅜	28.27	3,156.73	29,000	111,669.32
1957	1,000	30⅛	31.20	3,187.93	30,000	96,036.39
1958	1,000	48	20.83	3,208.76	31,000	154,020.48
1959	1,000	69½	14.34	3,223.10	32,000	222,796.78
1960	1,000	52	19.23	3,242.33	33,000	168,601.16

*Adjusted for 5-for-1 split in 1929.

time of his purchase in 1942, for example, he holds 2,274.52 shares, which cost him $15,000 and now have a market value of $11,372.65. But his average cost is only about a point and a half above the current market price of 5, so that a rise of that amount will be enough to give him a profit if he wishes to sell out.

It is interesting to note that *the dollar averaging principle automatically insures that most of the stock held will have been bought at bargain levels.* Without having to give any thought to the matter at all, the investor bought relatively few shares at the high levels of 1928 and 1929, and began to reduce his share purchases when the stock began its rise during the forties and fifties. This built-in caution at high prices is more or less typical of formula plans in general, but is especially notable in dollar averaging, and it works completely automatically. To see the effectiveness of this principle, note that the investor picked up more shares in the bargain year of 1942 alone than he did during the entire last decade of the plan—an example of shrewd investing that many a professional might envy!

Obviously, the case history has a happy ending, with the total $33,000 investment growing to nearly $170,000 by the end of 1960. This is, of course, partly a fortuitous result of the big bull market of the fifties, but even before it began, in 1950, our investor had a paper profit of *more than 100 percent, even though the stock had recovered to barely a fifth of its initial market price.*

"FULLY AUTOMATIC" PROFIT PRODUCER

Studying a few examples of this type of dollar averaging experience may give the reader the idea that it makes little difference whether a good stock or a bad stock is picked for the plan. Table 3, which charts the price history of two totally imaginary stocks, is evidence of this. Both Stock A and Stock B are followed through 10 regularly spaced buying points. Both stocks are at 100 at the beginning. The sum of $500 is invested in each stock at each purchase point, for a total investment in each of $5,000.

Stock A immediately goes into a sharp decline, falling to a low of 2, and recovers only a small amount of the loss, ending at 5. Stock B, on the other hand, rises 10 points between purchase points, to a high of 190 at the finish. Despite the difference between the two stocks, the plan involving the "dog" ends with a total market value of $7,650, as against only $6,830.50 for the "star performer."

TABLE 3

DOLLAR AVERAGING
Hypothetical Examples

$500 Periodic Investment in Each of Two Stocks.

| | | | STOCK A | | | | STOCK B | |
BUYING PERIOD	TOTAL AMOUNT IN- VESTED	PRICE	NO. SHARES PUR- CHASED	TOTAL NO. SHARES PUR- CHASED	TOTAL MKT. VALUE	PRICE	NO. SHARES PUR- CHASED	TOTAL NO. SHARES PUR- CHASED	TOTAL MKT. VALUE
1	$ 500	100	5	5	$ 500	100	5.00	5.00	$ 500.00
2	1,000	20	25	30	600	110	4.55	9.55	1,050.50
3	1,500	10	50	80	800	120	4.17	13.72	1,646.40
4	2,000	5	100	180	900	130	3.85	17.57	2,284.10
5	2,500	2	250	430	860	140	3.57	21.14	2,959.60
6	3,000	2	250	680	1,320	150	3.33	24.47	3,670.50
7	3,500	2	250	930	1,860	160	3.13	27.60	4,416.00
8	4,000	2	250	1,180	2,360	170	2.94	30.54	5,191.80
9	4,500	2	250	1,430	2,860	180	2.78	33.32	5,997.60
10	5,000	5	100	1,530	7,650	190	2.63	35.95	6,830.50

The key, again, is that as a stock drops, purchases made at the low points reduce the average cost so drastically that, eventually, only a small recovery suffices to produce relatively large profits. In the case of the steadily rising stock, the number of shares bought continues to decline at each purchase point, and reduces the chance for potential profit. (It should be emphasized that these examples are imaginary and were contrived for the express purpose of showing some of the less well-known aspects of dollar averaging, and to highlight the importance of continuing the plan, even though the outlook may seem dim.)

It is this tendency of dollar averaging to produce a profit under all kinds of circumstances that has led many observers to label it the "magic formula." Lucile Tomlinson calls it the "unbeatable formula," which comes close to being a highly accurate description.

The few critics of dollar averaging have uncovered so little to find fault with in the method that they usually confine themselves to pointing out that poor results can ensue if the investor happens to pick a poorly suited stock. One commentator showed that, although General Motors and Woolworth were rated equally by an investment advisory service in 1939, results of two plans, one based on each stock, showed a wide difference, with Woolworth limping in far behind.[3] Among stocks listed in another study as producing "mediocre results" were American Telephone and Telegraph, Pennsylvania Railroad and Coca-Cola.[4] Both these comments were made in early 1958. From that point to mid-1961, Woolworth, AT&T and Coca-Cola had all more than doubled. Most stocks give fairly good results *over a period of time*, and the chances of picking what will amount to a dollar-averaging "lemon" are not too great in actual practice.

If past markets are a guide to the future, it must be assumed that, carried out over a period of years, dollar averaging plans based on stocks moving with the market are invariably successful in producing a profit. Miss Tomlinson studied each of the 24 10-year periods beginning January 1 of each year between the beginning of 1920 and the end of 1952, and found that, based on plans using the Dow-Jones Industrials, there "was no 10-year period in all that time when at least a 25 percent gain over cost did not exist, either at the end of the accumulation period, or within five years afterward."[5] In 19 of the 24 test periods, in fact, there was a profit at the end, ranging from 2 to 110 percent. The policy of holding the stocks purchased during the 10 years for five more (with no new purchases) produced profits of 27 to 148 percent. This study covered all types of markets, some of the almost straight-up variety, others almost straight down.

HOW YOU CAN LOSE

All commentators on the subject agree that successful operation of a dollar averaging program requires (1) a firm decision at the outset to continue the plan over a considerable period, (2) the nerve to continue even when the outlook is blackest, and (3) some assurance that a steady flow of capital will be available.

In our RCA example, it was seen that in order to achieve the highly satisfactory results at the end of 20 years or more, it was necessary for the investor not only to put up with a paper loss for several years, beginning shortly after inauguration of the plan, but also to continue sinking money into what may have looked like a totally worthless stock in the depths of a depression.

This requirement that the plan be continued even when the outlook is black is the major weakness of dollar averaging—or perhaps it would be more accurate to say that this is the major weakness of the investor who uses dollar averaging. During the bear market of 1957-58, for example, which was certainly relatively mild in amplitude and short in duration, it was reported that "long-time users of dollar averaging are 'chucking it all' . . . For it's sometimes hard to know when you are showing foresight and when you are throwing good money after bad." [6] It is probable that some investors in this period were not only disgusted, but were broke, which is a condition not always susceptible to cure by will power. Naturally, stock bargains have a habit of occurring in periods when few potential customers have the means to pick them up, which is perhaps partly why they occur in the first place.

Even if it is necessary to trim purchases somewhat during times of economic stringency, it is advisable that the dollar averager keep up his program to the best of his ability. (Some institutions which use dollar averaging, not subject to the economic problems of the individual, follow a policy of stepping up purchases during periods of low prices, and shaving them in periods when the market is high. Such attempts to second-guess the market are not recommended. The danger is that the whole plan will be abandoned for the temporarily more exciting activity of calling market turns in advance.)

No one can predict, of course, how a market decline may affect him—financially or emotionally. But the would-be dollar averager should be prepared to face the problems and aggravations of a bear market when he starts his program, since it is highly probable that some discouraging slump will at least temporarily occur in any program scheduled to run for a number of years.

It is hardly surprising that dollar averaging has become immensely popular among investors. Currently, there are an estimated million or so active cumulative investment plans involving purchases of mutual funds. Even the Stock Exchange's Monthly Investment Plan, after a hesitant start in 1954 (it was characterized by one critic in 1955 as a "mistake" which was "falling on its face" [7]), and against the indifference of most brokerage houses, now boasts a roster of over 100,000 adherents.

It is possible to carry out a dollar averaging program with purchases planned on any regular, periodic basis, the most common being monthly, quarterly or annually. Any interval will produce results approximately comparable to any other, and the investor should choose whatever method is most convenient. If it is decided to operate the plan using a single common stock, commissions can be reduced by choosing quarterly rather than monthly payments, since—up to a certain point—larger purchases carry a lower commission, calculated as a percentage of total market value.

As to the type of security to choose, you may pick one or more common stocks, or the shares of a mutual fund. If you choose to buy common stocks, you will undoubtedly find it advantageous to use the Monthly Investment Plan, information about which can be obtained from many New York Stock Exchange member firms. In this plan, the investor receives full and fractional shares worth exactly the amount of his regular payment (monthly or quarterly only), and full and proportional fractional dividends are paid into his account (and automatically reinvested, if he likes).

The investor who uses this plan, however, comes in for some stiff commissions. On amounts under $100, he pays six percent, substantially more than that charged on larger purchases. On amounts of more than about $600, however, they drop to about two percent or below.

In view of the fact that individual stocks will give varying results under dollar averaging, it might be worth suggesting that the investor using MIP select at least three securities, buying shares of each every third month, thus obtaining a modicum of diversification.

More popular than the MIP are mutual fund accumulation plans. These, too, have high sales charges for the most part, but there are about 25 or so with no such charge. Examples are Scudder, Stevens & Clark Common, deVegh Investing Co., and Energy Fund. These have no salesmen, and are sold only through the mail. Complete details on those with a sales load can be obtained from most brokerage houses and mutual fund marketing organizations. One way to accomplish somewhat the same end as buying a mutual fund and yet reduce the sales charge is to buy shares of closed-end investment companies listed on the Stock Exchange. Among these are Lehman Corp., Tri-Continental Corp., and Madison Fund (formerly Pennroad). If purchases are over $200, the commission will be substantially smaller than the sales load of most open-end companies.

Mutual funds are ideally suited to dollar averaging. Plans can be set up calling for purchases of as little as $25 worth a month, and all details of security selection, record keeping, etc., are handled by management. Procedures for making the regular payments are as simple and uncomplicated as the regular payment of a telephone bill. They provide for purchases of fractional shares to fill out the exact amount invested, automatic reinvestment of dividends and/or capital gains distributions, and systematic periodic notification of the investor as to the status of his account and of his tax liability. Records of hypothetical dollar averaging programs are supplied by many of the funds in their sales literature, and results are generally satisfactory.

THREE

THE CONSTANT-DOLLAR PLAN

From this point on, all the formulas treated in this book deal with an established fund, rather than with a constant flow of new money to invest, as in the case of dollar averaging. However, just as dollar averaging can be adapted to the requirements of a fixed sum, so can most of these other plans be used in managing a fund which is constantly being added to. These techniques are all broadly classified as "ratio" formulas.

THE RATIO PRINCIPLE

Like dollar averaging, ratio plans are aimed at combating the danger of losses due to unforeseen fluctuations in the stock market. Ratio plans are all alike in that they are concerned solely with the proportion of the investor's capital which is held in stocks as against that used to purchase bonds. The percentage of stocks is intended to be increased when the market is low, and decreased when it is high. The idea is to reduce the amount of risk securities held when prices are high, and conversely to purchase stocks at what are presumed to be bargain levels when the market is low.

A couple of comments are in order concerning the practicability of these formulas for the average investor. First, it is hardly realistic to talk about techniques which involve the sale of a few hundred, or even a few thousand, dollars' worth of stocks in order to replace them with bonds. Most small investors (and a great many large investors) have neither sufficient knowledge of the bond market nor sufficient capital to make buying bonds a practical matter. For most investors, therefore, an indication to sell a certain amount of stocks and buy bonds with the proceeds can most effectively be interpreted as a direction to withdraw the specified amount of money from the stock market and divert it to a savings account or an account with a savings and loan association, or hold it in cash.

As will be made clear, the whole object of placing a portion of one's capital in "bonds" is to reduce the percentage of one's account that is subject to fluctuations. Obviously, bonds do fluctuate, with the interest rate cycle as well as with the financial condition of the issuer, but the ups and downs in the bond market tend to be much less pronounced than those in the stock market. However, the principal in a savings account is always guaranteed, can (generally) be converted into cash at any time, and usually earns a satisfactory rate of return. Most investors can make the same use of these formulas as large investors who actually do hold most of the fixed-interest portion of their portfolios in bonds. These larger investors cannot, of course, make any practical use of savings accounts, but they usually are able to use a combination of bonds, preferred stocks, commercial paper, bills and other fixed-interest investments to attain the desired degree of stability while still earning a satisfactory return on this portion of their portfolios.

Regardless of actual investor practice, the term "bonds" is consistently used in this book to refer to that part of the portfolio not subject to fluctuations, since this is the standard terminology in discussions of formulas, and the illustrative examples assume that this portion does not in fact fluctuate.

Some comment should also be made about the stock portion of the portfolio. This means all investments subject to substantial price risks—common stocks as well as convertible bonds and preferreds. The reader will note that the Dow-Jones Industrial Average or some other stock market index is used to indicate the movement of the market in the illustrative examples. There are several valid objections to this: the various stock averages are calculated according to different principles, all have imperfections, and none of them agree exactly with one another. Furthermore, even if the averages did indicate with any precision what the market is doing (which they don't), they certainly cannot be a reliable indicator of individual investor experience.

Nevertheless, it is necessary to have some indicator of stock market movements, and all the popular averages have proved themselves to be generally satisfactory for this purpose. And for the purpose of managing investments according to a formula, it is not the intention to find an indicator which will exactly match the investor's own results. The whole purpose of using an average is to indicate changes in the degree of risk through reference to changes in the level of the average. It may be assumed that if the market as a whole is subject to a high degree of risk, the stocks held by any particular investor will also be subject to a high degree of risk, no matter how unrelated the previous movement of these stocks might be to the movement of the average.

THE CONSTANT-DOLLAR PLAN

Simplest of all ratio formulas is the constant-dollar plan. Its terms dictate that a stated dollar amount of stocks will be held at all times. For example, the investor who has, say, $20,000 in total investment funds may decide on a figure of $10,000 as the amount of stocks he wishes to hold, which would leave $10,000 in the bond account. If the market goes up a specified percentage, stocks are sold to bring the stock account back to $10,000, and if the market declines by a similar amount, sufficient funds are transferred from the bond portion to the stock portion to boost stocks back to $10,000. This means that, although the *dollar value* of stocks always remains the same, the percentage of stocks held in the total account will drop as the market rises, and increase as the market declines. The implicit assumption here, of course, is that as the market moves up, it is that much more vulnerable, and the percentage of stocks should be reduced; as it drops, stocks are just that much more worth having.

No attempt is made, of course, to define what constitutes "high" or "low" points in terms of market averages. Shifts from stocks to bonds (or vice versa) can be indicated either by the actual change in the value of the stock portion of the account, or by a change in one of the popular market indexes. As discussed above, it is recommended that the signal be taken from an average, rather than from the value of the account, for two reasons: (a) changes in the value of an individual portfolio of

TABLE 4

CONSTANT-DOLLAR PLAN
Hypothetical Example

STOCK INDEX	VALUE OF PORTFOLIO BEFORE ADJUSTMENT STOCKS	BONDS	ADJUSTMENT	VALUE OF PORTFOLIO AFTER ADJUSTMENT BONDS	STOCKS
100.0	......	......	Begin Plan	$10,000	$10,000
120.0	$12,000	$10,000	Sell $2,000 stocks	10,000	12,000
144.0	12,000	12,000	Sell $2,000 stocks	10,000	14,000
172.8	12,000	14,000	Sell $2,000 stocks	10,000	16,000
207.4	12,000	16,000	Sell $2,000 stocks	10,000	18,000
165.9	8,000	18,000	Buy $2,000 stocks	10,000	16,000
132.7	8,000	16,000	Buy $2,000 stocks	10,000	14,000
106.2	8,000	14,000	Buy $2,000 stocks	10,000	12,000
85.0	8,000	12,000	Buy $2,000 stocks	10,000	10,000
68.0	8,000	10,000	Buy $2,000 stocks	10,000	8,000
54.4	8,000	8,000	Buy $2,000 stocks	10,000	6,000
65.3	12,000	6,000	Sell $2,000 stocks	10,000	8,000
78.4	12,000	8,000	Sell $2,000 stocks	10,000	10,000
94.1	12,000	10,000	Sell $2,000 stocks	10,000	12,000
100.0	10,627	12,000	......	....	....

stocks (especially if the portfolio is small) have far less significance in indicating the vulnerability of the market as a whole than an index of the whole market; (b) the task 'of calculating the value of a portfolio at frequent intervals could be a burdensome task, requiring an undue amount of attention.

Changes can be made either at the precise time a stated percentage advance or decline occurs in the stock portion of the account—say, 10 or 20 percent—or the account can be re-examined quarterly, semi-annually or annually—and the stock portion readjusted to its original figure. This latter procedure seems the more sensible approach. A study of a number of case histories of the method seems to indicate the advantages of checking up daily are negligible.

Table 4 presents a hypothetical constant-dollar plan followed over a complete market cycle. Starting with a total portfolio of $20,000, the investor puts $10,000 in both the bond and stock portions. With every 20 percent change in the market, he re-establishes the stock portion at the original amount by selling stock and buying bonds or vice-versa. (As the example is not based on actual market conditions, it is not possible to assume quarterly re-evaluations, even though this is the recommended procedure.) For simplicity's sake, we are assuming that the stocks in our investor's portfolio move exactly with the

39

market, even though—as mentioned earlier—this is unlikely in actual practice.

When the plan is begun, our hypothetical stock average is at 100. It rises to 207.4, then goes into a decline which takes it to 54.4, after which it rises again to 100. At the final point in the table, the average is brought up to 100, but no portfolio changes are made, since the average did not move a full 20 percent since the previous adjustment. Note that the investor did not profit to the full extent of the bull market, since the value of his portfolio rose to only $28,000—an increase of 40 percent —at the high point, while the market more than doubled. When the market fell, however, his bond position protected him to some extent, and his portfolio's value was $16,000 at the low point— only 20 percent below its original value—even though the market as measured by the average fell by slightly more than 45 percent.

Most important, however, is the final value of our investor's portfolio—$22,627, or a gain of about 13 percent. Commissions, not considered in the table, would have been about $365 on a round-lot basis for listed stocks, bringing the net increase in the portfolio's value to about 11.5 percent. This is not a bad gain, when you consider that the market as a whole is right back where it started from. If the portfolio had been invested in either all stocks or all bonds, there would have been no profit at all. But our investor managed to secure a respectable profit over the entire cycle merely by using a very simple formula.

Note that no *time* indications are given, or required, in a constant-dollar plan. Operation of a plan such as the one presented in the table might stretch over a period of many years, or be completed in only a fraction of that time. If the market fails to move 10 percent for an extended period, no changes need be made in the portfolio.

At the end of the plan, the stock portion of the portfolio— which stood at 50 percent at the start—has dropped to about 47 percent. This is not much, but with wider market swings, extending over a longer period, quite a discrepancy could develop. If it was reasonable for the investor to hold 50 percent of his funds in cash when the stock index stood at 100 at the beginning of the plan, is it not still logical to do so when the index returns to that figure? The investor can, of course, adjust his portfolio to a 50-50 figure when the change becomes considerable. A faithful follower of the constant dollar plan who began operations at an extremely low point of the market would find himself permanently frozen to an arbitrarily established dollar figure of stocks, and barred from participating to any great extent in bull markets. If he were to re-adjust the original percentage figure after, say, a substantial market rise, he would be putting himself in the position of market seer, which is the very thing a formula is supposed to avoid. Some authorities suggest certain percentage limitations on the amount of deviation from the original dollar figure which should be tolerated before a readjustment is made. For example, it might be specified that the original proportions be re-established when the percentage of stocks in the portfolio rises to 55 or drops to 45. Another suggestion is that the portfolio be readjusted to its original percentage division after a certain period of time—say three or four years. But such rules must of necessity be arbitrary and do not solve the central problem.

Another weakness of the constant-dollar plan is the problem of what to do with additional funds which may become available. In the example above, suppose our investor suddenly won $5,000 at the race track. Should he divide this among the two sections of his portfolio according to the original percentage he had set up, or should he use the current percentages as a guide? Or, since the money is surplus funds he wasn't counting on, should he commit it all to risk investments? Or, inasmuch as he has already decided how much money he wants to commit to equity investments, should he not add the entire sum to the bond portion? Such a difficulty does not destroy the value of the plan, but it can cause some confusion.

AN INFORMAL PLAN

Actually, the plan is an extremely informal one, and the disadvantages mentioned above are not terribly serious in practice. Investors who use such a plan are interested in getting some advantages of owning common stocks, without incurring undue risks, and the constant-dollar formula presents a practical approach. The amount of stocks to be held is a matter of individual preference. Our investor above could have chosen $5,000 as his stock proportion, just as well as $10,000.

Over a long period of time, the method produces satisfactory results. One study[1] shows results of a hypothetical test of the method over the 1926-1950 period, starting with a $10,000 fund, $5,000 of which was to be held in stocks, and using the Dow-Jones Industrials as an action indicator. Additional purchases are specified at every 20 percent decline in the Dow-Jones Industrials, and sales at every 25 percent advance. By the end of 1950, total value of the fund amounted to $15,773, and had produced an average yield of 5.46 percent over the total period. This capital appreciation of about 50 percent compares with a net rise of about 46 percent in the Dow-Jones Industrials. At the end of 1945, however, when the average had traced a complete market cycle and had returned only to the starting point, the constant-dollar portfolio gain already amounted to about 50 percent, and changed little in succeeding years.

In order to arrive at this result, the authors of the study (who are unenthusiastic about this formula) had to choose an extremely advantageous beginning date—1926. An investor who wants to begin a plan might reasonably not know whether the market is in fact at a suitable point. If it turns out that he began his plan at a market peak, then successive drops in the averages will dictate additional purchases of stock until he may have no funds remaining in the bond account with which to buy anything, which will relieve him of the task of calculating his position, but will not do his finances much good.

Actually, an investor who uses the constant-dollar plan is saying, *in effect*, that the point at which he begins is a "normal" market level, above which it is wise to sell some stocks, and below which it is advisable to purchase more stocks. Thus the formula presents a sizable obstacle at the very beginning, which is not easy to overcome. This, undoubtedly, is the most serious weakness of the constant-dollar method. (A partial solution to the problem appears in the following chapter.) It appears in some other formulas, too, but does not usually place such severe limitations on the plan's operations. On the plus side, however, it may be said that few periods in the market would have proved completely disastrous as a starting point.

Simplicity is the main feature of the plan, and it may appeal to some investors for that reason. It has the virtues of a methodical hedging against fluctuations in the market, which can be quite valuable, and at the same time the convenience of an essentially informal plan.

FOUR

THE CONSTANT-RATIO FORMULA

Somewhat similar to the constant-dollar plan is the constant-ratio formula. It is one of the oldest formulas in existence, having been used as long as 20 years ago. More important, it still stands up today, and is widely used, despite the drastic changes which have taken place in the market.

It fulfills, perhaps better than any other formula, the basic theoretical requirements of formula investing. It permits the investor to participate to some extent in bull markets, while at the same time protecting him from serious price declines. And because it is not married to a fixed-dollar amount in stocks (as in the constant-dollar plan) or a "norm" (as in the variable-ratio plans to be discussed in the next chapter), the method has a high degree of flexibility. One reason for its durability and its effectiveness is that no forecast whatsoever is made about the character of future markets, other than that they will continue to fluctuate, which is hardly a hazardous assumption.

Because of the clear-cut advantages of this plan, it has been widely used by institutions, such as trust, endowment and pension funds. Its first use, as will be seen later, was in a college endowment fund. In past years, however, its popularity with some institutional investors has waned (although others are still quite satisfied), and it has been adopted more and more by individuals.

Here is how it works: The total investment fund is divided into two equal portions, one half to be invested in stocks, the other in bonds. As the market rises, stocks are sold and bonds are bought to restore the 50-50 relationship. If the market goes down, the reverse procedure is followed, bonds being sold and stocks bought to return to the 50-50 ratio.

At first glance, it may seem that the plan is very similar to the constant-dollar formula, as described in the last chapter. The two plans do share some characteristics, of course, and the object of both is the same. But the constant-ratio plan does not present the investor with quite so many knotty decisions during its operation, and results over the long term have tended to be somewhat better.

As in the constant-dollar plan, the bond and stock portions of the account may be readjusted according to changes in the value of stocks held, or in a stock index. As before, the adjustments can be made as shifts of a certain specified minimum percentage occur, or at regular intervals. Here again, it is recommended that the investor make the necessary shifts of bonds and stocks at regular intervals. Studies show that this procedure produces good results—in addition, of course, to its greater convenience.

HOW IT OPERATES

The hypothetical example shown in Table 5 assumes the same fluctuations in the market index as in our constant-dollar example. A $20,000 account is assumed, with a 50-50 ratio between stocks and bonds, and the account is readjusted with

TABLE 5
CONSTANT-RATIO PLAN
Hypothetical Example

STOCK INDEX	VALUE OF PORTFOLIO BEFORE ADJUSTMENT		ADJUSTMENT	VALUE OF PORTFOLIO AFTER ADJUSTMENT	
	STOCKS	BONDS		STOCKS	BONDS
100.0	. . . . . .	. . . . . .	Begin Plan	$10,000	$10,000
120.0	$12,000	$10,000	Sell $1,000 stocks	11,000	11,000
144.0	13,200	11,000	Sell $1,100 stocks	12,100	12,100
172.8	14,520	12,100	Sell $1,210 stocks	13,310	13,310
207.4	15,971	13,310	Sell $1,330 stocks	14,641	14,641
165.9	11,713	14,641	Buy $1,464 stocks	13,177	13,177
132.7	10,542	13,177	Buy $1,318 stocks	11,859	11,859
106.2	9,487	11,859	Buy $1,186 stocks	10,673	10,673
85.0	8,538	8,538	Buy $1,063 stocks	9,601	9,601
68.0	7,681	9,601	Buy $ 960 stocks	8,641	8,641
54.4	6,913	8,641	Buy $ 778 stocks	7,691	7,691
65.3	9,229	7,691	Sell $ 769 stocks	8,460	8,460
78.4	11,152	8,460	Sell $ 846 stocks	9,306	9,306
94.1	11,167	9,306	Sell $ 931 stocks	10,237	10,237
100.0	10,878	10,237	. . . .	. . . .	. . . .

every 20 percent rise or decline in the stock index. The stock index rises from 100 to 207.4, falls to 54.4, and climbs back to 100, thus completing the market cycle. (At the last stage shown, no readjustment takes place, since the index has not risen a full 10 percent from the last adjustment point.)

At the end of the complete market cycle, the total value of the portfolio is $21,115. Commissions, not figured in the example, would have amounted to about $230 on the basis of round-lot transactions in listed stocks, leaving our investor with a net profit after commissions of $885, or just under five percent of the starting value of his portfolio. This profit is less than half that produced by the constant-dollar plan under the same conditions. Does that mean the constant-dollar plan is better? The answer is no. A close look at the two tables shows that, at the high point (when the average stood at 207.4), the constant-ratio portfolio has a market value of $29,281, against only $28,000 for the constant-dollar portfolio. Furthermore, it is obvious that the constant-ratio portfolio would continue to benefit in larger measure from any subsequent market rise, since its portfolio contains over $15,000 in stocks, while the constant-dollar portfolio has stocks worth only $10,000.

At the low point touched by the average (54.4), the constant-ratio formula's portfolio is worth only $15,554, while that of the constant-dollar portfolio has a value of $16,000. However, any further decline in the stock market would do much more damage to the constant-dollar portfolio than to the constant-ratio portfolio, since the amount of stocks held in the constant-dollar portfolio must remain the same, while the percentage of bonds —which are intended to provide protection against falling stock prices—will continue to shrink.

A LESS FLEXIBLE PLAN

The point is that the constant-dollar plan is far less flexible than the constant-ratio, and far less able to function well under changing market conditions. If you could be certain that the market would always trace a complete cycle of the type postulated in our example, then you could choose the constant-dollar plan with assurance that you were making the right choice. It is doubtful that such an opinion would be very reliable, however.

Another comparison of the two methods was made over the 1926-1950 period. Using essentially the same method of shifting funds between accounts, a $10,000, 50-50 constant-ratio plan would end up with a profit of $5,839, compared with $5,773 for the constant-dollar. Were the test examples to be continued a few more years into the fifties, the constant-ratio plan would pull even farther ahead, due to its built-in advantage in a rising market. This would be especially significant in this case, because by the end of the test the constant-dollar formula is only about 30 percent in stocks, while the constant-ratio plan is still at 50 percent.

AUTOMATICALLY ADAPTIVE

It might be worth pointing out that, since the long-term trend of the American economy has always been irregularly upward, the constant-ratio plan promises to be able to adjust itself to this gradual rise somewhat better than the constant-dollar plan. Naturally, the uptrend is subject to frequent declines or periods of stagnation—sometimes of considerable duration—but the upward movement has always reasserted itself in time. The constant-ratio plan provides some protection during these periods of decline, while continually adapting itself automatically to changing market conditions.

Lucile Tomlinson presents results of a series of five hypothetical constant ratio plans, each covering 11 years in the 55-year period 1897-1951.[2] This study includes a varied assortment of markets. Adjustments were made on a once-a-year basis, no adjustment to be made unless a certain specified percentage of upward or downward movement in the market had occurred. In three of the periods, the constant-ratio formula turned in a significantly better performance than did a "buy and hold" plan (i.e., a portfolio consisting of half bonds and half stocks at the start of each period, with no adjustments of proportions during the plan), and in the other two fell only slightly behind.

The best profit performance of the constant-ratio plan showed up in the 1919-1920 period, with a gain of 89.4 percent. The worst was in the 1930-1940 period, which produced a loss of 12.7 percent (the Dow-Jones Industrials dropped 47 percent in the same span of time). Miss Tomlinson concludes that the best results are produced by the constant-ratio formula "when stock prices fluctuate over a fairly wide range but there is no extreme in either direction."

HOW DO YOU START?

Before beginning a constant-ratio plan, there are two decisions the investor must make. First, there is the problem of what ratio to adopt. In the examples referred to so far, a 50-50 ratio has been used, and in fact the plan is sometimes called the "equalizing" formula, because the stock and bond portions are "equalized" periodically.

But there is no reason to stick to the 50-50 ratio. Some conservative investors prefer a higher percentage of bonds, and the more venturesome choose a higher percentage of stocks. The investor who can afford the risk will still obtain some of the advantages of using the formula method even if he hikes the stock percentage to 75 percent, and will profit more in case the market heads upward. And the investor who decides to use a higher percentage of bonds will get the advantage of equity investments—protected to some extent by his use of the formula method—while maintaining a higher degree of safety because of the larger bond portion of his account.

Another problem to be met is the question of when to start the plan. As in the case of the constant-dollar method, the level of the market at which the plan is begun is of no small importance. The effect on final results will not be as great as in the constant-dollar method, since the constant-ratio plan is continually adjusting the amount of stocks held as the market shifts.

One study, comparing plans with various starting dates, points up the importance of this.[8] A hypothetical fund started in 1935 shows a profit immediately, while an account begun in 1930 shows an immediate loss and takes about 15 years to move into a profit position.

Obviously, the investor can never be sure whether the market level at any particular time will turn out to be high or low, and there is no ready answer to the problem of the starting date. If the investor who wants to use a constant-ratio formula is to be expected to predict the future direction of the market, then the formula method is not as "automatic" as its supporters claim, and if he is capable of making such a prediction, he doesn't need a formula.

One solution is to combine the constant ratio plan with a dollar averaging approach. Assuming a 50-50 stock-bond ratio has been decided on, 10 percent of the account can be invested in stocks immediately, say, with the account being treated as a 10-90 constant-ratio plan for the first year, after which time the account is adjusted to a 20 percent position in stocks. After another year, the account is adjusted again to a 30-70 proportion, and so on, until it reaches the 50-50 point, in four years. This would not necessarily mean buying exactly the same dollar amount of stocks each time, since market fluctuations would inevitably change the percentages between adjustment points. Let us assume, for example, the investor starts with a $10,000 fund, and buys $1,000 of stocks and $9,000 of bonds. After a year, when he is ready to re-adjust, the market has gone up 10 percent, bringing the value of his stockholdings to $1,100, which makes his total account $10,100. He now adjusts to a 20 percent stock position, or $2,020 of stocks. Since he already holds $1,100 of stocks, he buys $920 more, leaving the bond account at $8,080.

The intervals and percentages used above are arbitrary, of course, and can easily be modified by the investor to suit his own preferences. But this procedure is a solution—and a workable one—although it does delay getting the formula into full swing for some time. The previous chapter on dollar averaging demonstrated the practicality and good results of the technique, and the procedure outlined here is actually the dollar averaging approach applied to a fixed sum of money, except that it stops before putting the investor entirely into stocks. It will be recalled that this was precisely the procedure the New Mexico Investment Council selected for the investment of its Permanent Fund. Only 25 percent of the total portfolio was to be invested in common stocks, with a specific amount to be so invested each month over a period until the 25 percent proportion was reached. After that time, the portfolio was presumably to be operated as a 25-75 constant ratio plan.

Adding new funds to a constant-ratio fund presents no appreciable problems. They may be added at one of the adjustment dates, half in bonds and half in stocks, or added slowly, using a dollar averaging approach.

IMPROVING PROFIT PERFORMANCE

Many other such gimmicks have been suggested for improving results of the formula, but most of them were derived for the purpose of boosting profits during a market period that was already past. There is no reason to believe the improvements cannot be worked out (the writer has one of his own, in fact, which will be unveiled in the final chapter), but most of the trickery that has been used is very much like telling the investor to sell out just before a market break, without letting him in on the secret of when the market breaks are supposed to occur. This type of thing led one caustic commentor on modifications of formulas to observe that they "can reintroduce the principal opportunities for capital and income gain only to the extent to which they permit the return through a back entrance of the 'forecasting element' which they earlier let out through the front door." [4]

The constant-ratio formula can, of course, be modified at will to fit individual needs. One such modified plan was tested on the period from Jan. 31, 1943, to Jan. 31, 1951, a more or less arbitrary set of dates. [5] A $100,000 fund was assumed, established with 33 percent in stocks (since that was the approximate percentage of stocks held in trust funds at the starting date).

The rule for making shifts specified that the market must move 20 percent before a shift would be made. The unusual twist is added by a rule that the original percentage is not to be re-established at the adjustment point, but that if the trend is up, only enough stocks are sold to bring the stock portion down to 36 percent, and if the trend is down, only enough are brought to bring it up to 30 percent. If the trend still goes in the same direction, the next shift will move the stock percentage to 39 percent or 27 percent, depending on direction of the trend. No further upward or downward percentage adjustments are made, if the market continues in the same direction, but at each transfer date thereafter, the 39 percent or 27 percent figure is still observed, but now at every 10 percent move in the market, instead of at 20 percent. But when the market *reverses* its trend, by at least 20 percent, then the original 33 percent figure for stocks is re-established, and the plan starts all over again.

During the period tested, the total $100,000 account grew to $130,319, while the Dow-Jones Industrials were increasing by over 80 percent. The formula is a conservative one, but does have the advantage of allowing larger purchases of stocks in a wide bull swing. This plan indicates the many variations that may be introduced in the constant ratio principle to suit varying preferences.

YALE AND KENYON

The first widely publicized use of the constant-ratio formula —in the late thirties—was the "Yale Plan," so-called because Yale University managed a part of its endowment fund according to the formula. The fund was started with stocks at 30 percent. If the stocks held advanced to a point where their total value amounted to 40 percent of the total fund, they were cut back to 35 percent. If an advance in stocks again brought the figure up to 40 percent, stocks were to be cut back again to 35 percent. If the market declined—at the beginning of the plan or otherwise—to as low as 15 percent, they were to be brought up to 20 percent.

The plan was subsequently revised at various times to allow for more fluctuations in stock prices, but the principle remained essentially the same, and resembled somewhat the modified plan discussed above, where ratios are adjusted in order to take advantage of trends continuing in the same direction over a long period of time. Yale apparently had fairly satisfactory results with the plan, but has in recent years changed it to such an extent that the University can now be said to have all but abandoned the formula method.

Kenyon College, however, also an early user of formulas, is still using the original plan, but the one it uses has never been, strictly speaking, a formula at all, since its investment committee has always felt free to depart from the plan whenever such a course seemed advisable. The ratio used is 40 percent in stocks, the remainder in bonds, and the plan is not to buy any stocks when the percentage is above 40, or to sell any when the percentage is below 40. When or whether to adjust the portfolio is up to the committee. Investment results have been highly satisfactory since the formula was first adopted about 20 years ago.

Undoubtedly the widest use of the constant-ratio plan is in large investment portfolios managed by trust departments of commercial banks and investment counselors. Many such investment professionals specify when a management contract is agreed to that the account will contain certain percentages of stocks and bonds, the exact figures depending on the needs of the client. In some cases, adjustments are not made by buying or selling securities already in the portfolio, but only in the disposition of new money which is added from time to time. The obvious advantage of this method under such circumstances is that both the portfolio manager and the client have a clear understanding of the principles according to which the portfolio is to be managed, which can help prevent disputes from arising. This, of course, is in addition to the investment advantages of the technique.

The fact that so many institutions have used the constant-ratio formula—even on an informal basis—is evidence of the valuable guidance that this investment technique can give.

FIVE

VARIABLE-RATIO FORMULAS

The progression from constant-ratio formulas to variable ratios is completely logical. Once an investor understands the principles of constant-ratio planning, he might well wonder about the feasibility of adding some flexibility to a formula by increasing the ratio of common stocks when the market is low, and cutting back when the market is high, thus maximizing purchases of stock at low prices and minimizing risks at high levels.

This is precisely what the variable-ratio plans attempt to do. Understanding the objective is easy—attaining it is somewhat less so. There have undoubtedly been more variable-ratio plans invented than any other type, and a high percentage of them have wound up in the ashcan. Some worked extraordinarily well over a period of time, and then became worthless because of changing conditions in the market. Others were obsolete almost as soon as devised. But variable ratios are by no means dead. On the contrary, at the present time there are probably more formulas of this type in use than any other.

Unfortunately, most of these plans can be used with difficulty, if at all, by the average investor. A good many of them have proved themselves to be of little value, and some of the others are either based on information which is not made public or require more work than most investors care to expend. However, they are presented here for the sake of completeness and to provide the reader with some possible sources of ideas which he may be able to apply to his own investing.

The major snag that variable-ratio inventors run into is the difficulty of deciding what are "low" and "high" markets. The whole success of the technique depends on a more or less successful advance charting of market levels, although it is a general assumption about the future range of prices that is made—not a precise prediction.

In view of statements earlier in this book about the difficulty of forecasting stock prices, the necessity to do so in variable-ratio plans may seem contradictory. But the difference between the type of assumptions made in these plans about the market and a definite prediction might be compared with the difference between assuming a general range of temperature in New York City over the coming year and making a flat prophecy about how hot it will be at 3 p.m. next Tuesday.

Although methods for determining high and low markets vary from formula to formula, the operating principles are similar in all. In all of them, a "median" or "norm" (the terms are substantially identical, and are used interchangeably in this book) is determined, which refers to a "normal" level of stock prices, as measured by a stock average. Above this it is assumed that the market is on progressively more dangerous ground, and that below it, stocks are increasingly undervalued. Therefore, all variable-ratio formulas call for successive sales of stock above the median, and purchases below. Perhaps a clearer idea can be obtained from the following diagram, which will serve as a general depiction of variable-ratio plans (Figures below the line refer to the stock-bond ratios):

75% BELOW MEDIAN	50% BELOW MEDIAN	25% BELOW MEDIAN	MEDIAN	25% ABOVE MEDIAN	50% ABOVE MEDIAN	75% ABOVE MEDIAN
80-20	70-30	60-40	50-50	40-60	30-70	20-80

The point on the diagram marked "Median" would indicate the "normal" level of the market, and would correspond to some figure—or range—in a market average. As shown, at this point the portfolio is to consist of half bonds and half common stocks. When the average rises 75 percent above the median, the proportion of stocks is to drop to 20 percent of the portfolio, and bonds rise to 80 percent. At the other points, the percentages of stocks and bonds are supposed to follow the indicated figures. This diagram is intended to give a general picture, and is not based on any particular formula.

The idea of increasing or decreasing the proportion of stocks (as the market crosses a predetermined point or moves into or out of a fixed "zone") applies to all variable-ratio formulas. The 50-50 proportion specified at the median can be changed, according to the needs and tastes of the investor, with other proportionate changes up and down the scale. For example, an investor willing to build more risk into his plan might fix a 65 percent proportion of stocks at the median, ranging from 35 percent at high market levels to 95 percent at the lows.

Variable-ratio plans differ in specifying whether portfolio shifts are to be made when the market enters a "zone" of predetermined width, or when it crosses a point fixed in advance to signal a new stock-bond relationship. In any case, when the market average is between two action points—or within the limits of a zone—the portfolio is to be handled as under a constant-ratio plan, with the ratios determined by the rules of the variable-ratio formula. In the case of the "action point" method, where a ratio shift is indicated by a crossing of the point by a market average, different ratios are specified for the same market level, depending on whether the market crossed the point in an uptrend or a downtrend. This will become clearer as we examine some examples of variable ratios.

Another point on which plans differ is the question of the so-called "halfway rule." This rule stipulates that no purchases or stocks are to be made above the median, and no sales of stocks are to be made below it. For example, in a hypothetical plan based on the diagram above, if the market average happened to rise 75 percent above the median, calling for a 20/80 stock-bond proportion, enough stocks would be sold to bring the percentage of stocks down to 20 percent. If the average were then to fall to 50 percent above the median, theoretically calling for a 30/70 relationship, no stocks would be bought to bring the stock portion of the account up to the indicated 30 percent, if the halfway rule were in operation. No stock would be bought, in fact, unless the market average fell to the median, at which time the stock percentage would be brought up to 50 percent all at once.

Apparently the original purpose of this rule was to allow a wide swing in stock prices to run for some time before the investor started chasing it. This would have been a good idea in the 1929-32 crash, when stocks bought even at levels long after the top turned out to have been purchased too soon. But rigorous application of the rule would prevent the investor from taking advantage of any intermediate-term fluctuations in prices. The 1957 market break, for example, carried the Dow-Jones Industrials down less than 20 percent, but the low point represented an excellent opportunity to buy stocks. A serious weakness of the halfway rule is that it tends to immobilize the account for long periods. It is generally agreed that the halfway rule is of little or no value over a period of time, and does at least as much harm to profits as it does good.

As in previously discussed formulas, portfolio changes from stocks to bonds or vice versa may be made at the precise time when the stock index gives a signal, or periodic examination may be made to determine if a change is indicated. Again, the practice of regularly spaced checks is recommended.

Variable-ratio plans fall into three general categories, classified by the method of determining the median. These are (a) trend-line plans, (b) moving-average plans and (c) intrinsic-value plans. All have proved to be workable at one time or another. Trend line plans have fallen in prestige over the past several years, but the other two continue to be used.

THE VASSAR PLAN

The Vassar Plan, although originally a moving average plan, changed so often while it was in use that it really fits in no single category, and was finally abandoned altogether. However, it was the first variable-ratio formula plan ever to receive wide publicity, is relatively simple in its principles, and will serve as a general introduction to the subject of variable ratios.

The plan was conceived in 1938 at a time when investors were still mindful of the dismal market experiences of the 1929 and 1937 declines. To begin with, the plan was based on "the monthly mean price of the Dow-Jones Industrial Average for the years 1930-38," which was 136.15.[1] Therefore, 135 was taken as the median. The percentages of stocks and bonds to be held in the account were to be adjusted after each 10-point drop from this median, and after each 15-point rise. The exact percentages were as follows:

DJIA	STOCKS	BONDS
105	100.00%	. . .
115	83.3	16.7%
125	66.7	33.3
135	50	50
150	37.5	62.5
165	25	75
180	12.5	87.5
195	. . .	100

Adjustments were made only if the market crossed an action point going *away from* the median, which is another way of saying that the halfway rule was to be followed: no purchases of stocks above the median, no sales below.

The plan assumed, on the one hand, that the market would continue to follow a path similar to the one it traced during the 1930-38 period, but on the other hand it ignored the fact that the Dow-Jones average fell to around 40 in 1932, which is more than 60 percent below the maximum-stock position provided for. Oddly enough, however, the market limits in the plan—105 and 195—turned out to be remarkably close to actual experience for several years. The fund was fully invested in stocks at the low of about 90 in 1942, and was completely in bonds at the high of 212 in 1946. From that point on, the plan ceased to function at all well.

Actually, it was modified during this period to be based on a 10-year moving average of the market index, but the outer limits remained the same. The main difficulty with the formula, clearly, was that the median—and therefore the maximum point at which stocks could be held—was much too low. Also, the restrictions placed on operation of the fund by the halfway rule prevented taking advantage of the fluctuations of the 1947-1949 period, during which time a few profits could have been snagged even though the plan was essentially wrong. The median was moved up to 145 when it became apparent that the fund was being paralyzed by the formula, but this didn't help because the market never fell that far.

Finally, the old formula was given up entirely, and a new method worked out. This was based on an arithmetic trend, i.e., a trend line drawn on an arithmetic-scale chart of the average, following the general direction of market movement over the years. Since this moved the median only up to 160 (the market missed dropping this low by less than two points in 1949), it was not very effective in improving the formula.

The upshot of Vassar's experience was that the formula method was thrown out entirely, and the investment advisors of the fund now depend exclusively on their judgment. At last report,[2] the college had 44.3 percent of its endowment in common stocks, a proportion presumably decided upon independently of mechanical rules.

TREND LINE FORMULAS

Probably the best-known formula plan ever devised is the Keystone 7-Step Plan, shown in Chart 1. When the 7-Step Plan was first devised in 1941 by Robert Warren, the channel lines

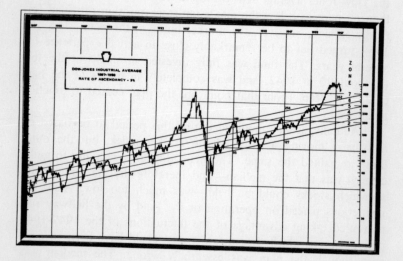

CHART 1: The original Keystone channel, based on observed growth of the Dow-Jones Industrial Average from 1897 to 1941. (Supplied by Keystone Custodian Funds.)

drawn on a logarithmic-scale chart of the Dow-Jones Industrial Average from 1897 to that year produced an almost perfect fit. It appeared that the upper and lower limits established by these channel lines conformed fairly well with the upper and lower limits of actual market fluctuations, and that the rate of growth of the lines—3 percent annually—was close to what had been the actual secular growth of market prices. The high point of 1929 and the low of 1932 were the only deviations, but this period was felt to be a freak, and not likely to occur.

The channels between the lines form "zones," and the operating principles of the formula dictated that specific proportions of stocks and bonds were to be held in each zone—progressively smaller percentages of stocks in the upper zones, and progressively larger percentages in the lower zones. It will be noted that the upper and lower limits of each zone change constantly from year to year.

As is shown on the chart, the Dow-Jones index rose beyond the upper limit of the channel in 1953, dictating a maximum bond position, and the formula has been largely frozen to the minimum percentage of stocks ever since. Mr. Warren wrote in 1953 that the channel lines should not be redrawn until it was proved that they were wrong.[3] In 1957, new channel lines were in fact set up to give a choice of three different growth rates on which to base his portfolio changes.

The second channel, shown in Chart 2, (*see p.* 60) uses the secular trend beginning in 1934, the year the dollar was devalued and the U.S. ecenomy became a much more money-managed one than had previously been the case. This channel extrapolates a growth rate of 4.4 percent a year.

The third channel is shown in Chart 3, (*see p.* 61) and begins in 1946, the year of the Employment Act, which sets forth the official U.S. policy of promoting economic growth and full employment. The growth rate is 8.8 percent a year.

In the brochure explaining the later channels, Keystone refers to the original channel as being suitable for the "conservative" investor, the second for the "middle-of-the-road" investor, and the last for the "optimistic" (or perhaps more speculative) investor.

The investor who wishes to use a formula can thus fit himself into either of the three categories that he feels best describes his investment attitude. He has no assurance that the channel he picks will prove to be the right one, however.

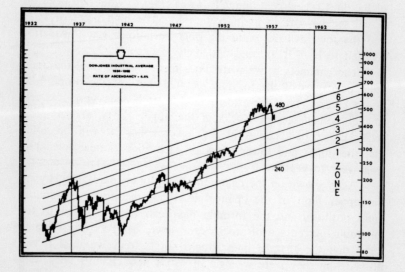

CHART 2: Revised Keystone channel, based on the growth rate of the DJIA from 1933 to 1957. (Supplied by Keystone Custodian Funds.)

All three plans are alike in that they set up a system of seven "zones"—five precisely marked off between the upper and lower channel limits, plus one each for the areas above and below the channel. Table 6 shows the zone limits for each of the three channels for 1959 and 1960. Notice that the formula does not use a median, as such, but a middle zone which is presumed to be "normal." A definite stock-bond relationship is established for each zone, but here, too, the investor is given a choice. Table 7 presents three sample proportion schedules for the various zones. A 7-Step planner thus can choose among three growth rates, as well as among three portfolio schedules, depending on the risks he is willing to assume.

The operating rules, as explained by Keystone, are numerous, but are the same no matter which of the plans is adopted.

TABLE 6

DJIA ZONE LIMITS
on the Three Keystone 7-Step Plans, 1959-60

ZONE	PLAN 1 "CONSERVATIVE" 1959	1960	PLAN 2 "MIDDLE-OF-THE-ROAD" 1959	1960	PLAN 3 "OPTIMISTIC" 1959	1960
7	Above 363	Above 374	Above 502	Above·524	Above 712	Above 770
6	317-362	326-273	438-501	457-523	621-711	672-769
5	276-316	284-325	381-437	398-456	541-620	585-671
4	240-275	247-283	332-380	346-397	471-540	509-584
3	209-239	215-246	289-331	301-345	410-470	443-508
2	182-208	188-214	252-288	263-300	357-409	386-442
1	Below 181	Below 187	Below 251	Below 262	Below 356	Below 385

The zones are numbered from 1 to 7, going from bottom to top. Zone 1 takes in all the area below the channel, and zone 7 all

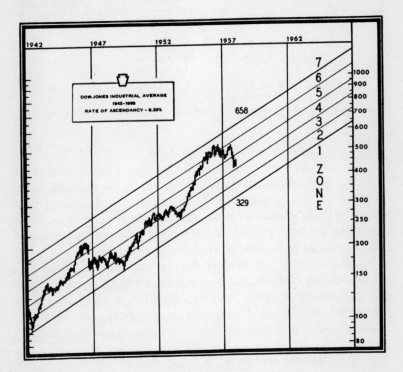

CHART 3: Third Keystone channel, based on growth rate from 1946 to 1957. (Supplied by Keystone Custodian Funds.)

the area above it. Zone 4 is the middle area. To begin the plan, it is necessary to know not only the current position of the Dow-Jones average, but also its history since it last moved out of Zone 4. If the average is in Zone 5, 6 or 7 (the three top zones) when the plan is initiated, "the account should start with the maximum" bond position required in the "highest zone reached since the average last crossed up through Zone 4." In other words, if the average is in Zone 5, but has arrived there by

TABLE 7

PROPORTION SCHEDULE
for Keystone 7-Step Plans
Percentages of Bonds and Stocks to Be Held in Various Zones.

ZONE	SCHEDULE 1 BONDS/STOCKS	SCHEDULE 2 BONDS/STOCKS	SCHEDULE 3 BONDS/STOCKS
7 (Top)	90/10	80/20	70/30
6	80/20	70/30	65/35
5	65/35	60/40	57/43
4	50/50	50/50	50/50
3	35/65	40/60	43/57
2	20/80	30/70	35/65
1 (Bottom)	10/90	20/80	30/70

rising out of the middle zone, into Zone 7, and back down, the stock-bond ratio will be that of Zone 7, not Zone 5 (this is, of course, the operating procedure specified by the halfway rule). Similarly, if the average is in Zone 1, 2 or 3, the account must begin with the maximum stock position called for by "the lowest zone reached since the market last crossed down through Zone 4." If the average is in Zone 4 when the plan is launched, however, the ratios depend on whether the market is falling or rising: if the average *rose* into the middle zone, the stock portion should be the maximum stock position called for in the lowest zone previously reached by the average; if the average *declined* into Zone 4, the bond position should be that of the highest zone reached.

Adjustments are made, if called for, at regular quarterly reviews of the account. But the halfway rule is called into service, and no stock purchases are made if the average is above Zone 4, and no sales if the average is below. No action is ever taken while the average is in Zone 4. When the halfway rule prevents selling or buying action, the plan is operated as a constant ratio formula, with the ratio of the last operative zone requirement.

A test of the plan, starting in 1941, when the original channel was first devised, and ending in 1951, was made by Miss Tomlinson,[4] with altogether remarkable results. At the end of the 11-year period, value of the account had increased by 81 percent, not counting income. The plan dictated buying stocks heavily at the 1942 low, holding them until the end of 1945, when substantial stock sales were made, thus getting largely out of stocks before the 1946 decline. And some advantage was taken of the fluctuations during the 1947-49 period. When the plan ended, the account was in Zone 6.

Unfortunately, the period during which the plan could show good results ended just around 1951, and if an account had been held intact, the minimum stock position would have been adopted soon after and no further stock purchases would have been permitted. The plan thus would have missed the big bull market of the fifties.

In the first plan, the top zone was reached in 1953, and the trend lines, even though they are moving gradually upward, have still not caught up. In the second plan, the market moved into the top zone about 1955, and has declined below the upper trend line only infrequently since. The market has been below the upper trend line of the third plan for quite long periods.

A glance at Table 6 will show that in both the first and second plans, an account operated under this formula now (late 1959) would be in the minimum stock position. In the third plan, it would be in Zone 6.

Naturally, the Keystone plan came in for some severe criticism when it became fairly apparent that the original channel was obsolete. Considering the unrepresentative nature of the Dow-Jones Index, some commentators were inclined to look on the whole principle as mere hocus-pocus, and the channel lines as so much coincidental doodling on graph paper misinterpreted as some sort of inevitable correlation.

Keystone Custodian Funds is a mutual fund sponsor, and its formula was originally publicized as a help in selling its own mutual funds. Keystone now places little faith in formula plans, and does not emphasize its channels in selling mutual funds.

There are other trend line formulas, but it would be impossible to cover them all. A well-known example is the Oberlin College plan, which established an arithmetic growth trend of about 2.7 points a year in the Dow-Jones Industrials. The trend lines of this plan turned out to be too low, and the formula was abandoned in 1955.[5]

MOVING AVERAGE FORMULAS

The moving average idea is highly logical, but the results that come from it are somewhat less than brilliant. The basic principle is to construct a median from an average of the positions of the market for the past several years. Every time a new year is included in the average, an old year is dropped off. For example, assume that a 10-year moving average is to be constructed in 1961. Take the previous 10 years—from 1951 through 1960, and average the means of the market average for each of the years. Next year, add the 1961 figure, and drop off 1951. Thus the average "moves," and gradually shows the effects of any changes.

The median in a moving average formula works like any other median. This is, lines are set up at intervals of, say, 10 or 15 percent intervals away from the median, which represent points at which the portfolio is to be adjusted.

The principle is admirable, and it seems reasonable to expect that a moving average would, by reflecting the ups and downs of a 10-year period, strike more or less a balance between the extremes, and that this would serve well as a basis for a formula timing plan. Unfortunately, it doesn't quite work out this way in practice.

Tests have been conducted on moving averages of various durations, and the conclusion appears to be that none of them work too well. The shorter the average is, the more violently it swings. The longer it is, the less it fluctuates, and therefore it adjusts to recent changes in the market too slowly.

One moving average formula that has proved itself to be fairly good, however, is the DuPont Institutional Plan, developed in 1947. It was devised by the research department of Francis I. DuPont & Co., a stock exchange house.[6]

The plan is more complex than most formulas. The median is a 120-month moving average of the monthly mean prices of the Dow-Jones Industrial Average. While it may seem that it is somewhat similar to the moving averages discussed above, and thus shares their weaknesses, the average is actually much more effective. The large number of series serves to flatten out the fluctuations which cause such serious dislocations of other moving averages. On the other hand, it must follow the market, since new market levels are constantly being included in the median.

The buying and selling techniques are unique. When the market rises 10 percent, stock is sold, as in some other plans, but the amount sold is not a fixed amount for each new stage of the market. It amounts to 10 percent of the proportion of stocks held at the previous adjustment point. Similarly, when the market drops 10 percent, 10 percent of bonds held at the last reshuffling are sold and the proceeds invested in stocks. (As set up by the DuPont firm, however, a rise is not treated in the same way as a decline, and bonds are sold at each 9.1 percent drop in the stock market, due to what is referred to as "percentage equivalents." What this does is make a 10 percent rise from one level to another exactly equal to a 10 percent drop from the lower level to the higher. For example, a 10 percent decline from 100 is 10, putting the average at 90, but a 10 percent rise would bring it back to only 99. The "percentage equivalent" takes care of this discrepancy.)

The halfway rule, forbidding sales of stock below the median and purchases above, is included in the plan's ground rules.

Another unusual rule is incorporated. If stock purchases are indicated in a falling market, stocks are not bought until the market has risen for two consecutive months, i.e., until the monthly mean price of the Dow-Jones for one month is above that for the preceding month. And if stock sales are called for in a rising market, the sales are made only when the average has fallen for two consecutive months.

The plan worked well at least to the early fifties. DuPont constructed a hypothetical model of an account using the plan, running from 1895 to the end of 1954, in which an initial investment of $1 million grew to over $10 million, not including dividends and interest.

INTRINSIC-VALUE TECHNIQUES

The category of variable-ratio plans generally known as "intrinsic value" formulas are without doubt the most sophisticated of all the formula investing techniques. For this reason they are also the most complicated, some of them so much so that they offer little practical guidance to the investor who manages his own portfolio.

Perhaps the simplest of all the intrinsic value formulas is one based on the "central value" method devised by Benjamin Graham, beyond all doubt the most brilliant security analyst in the U.S. The method is presented in his book, *The Intelligent Investor*.[7] It calls for dividing the average earnings on the Dow-Jones Industrials for the past 10 years by twice the current interest rate on Moody's high-grade (Aaa) bonds, and multiplying the resulting figure by 100. Mr. Graham does not actually recommend using the central value as the foundation of a variable ratio formula, but simply as a practice of selling all stocks when the DJIA reaches 120 percent of the central value, and buying back when it dips to 80 percent of the central value. Tests of this technique's practicality have produced excellent results, although, as Mr. Graham points out, "the intervals between signals have at times been so long as to try the investor's patience." A test of the method over the 1924-1953 period showed only seven points at which action is to be taken. The investor who followed the technique would have been out of the market completely from October, 1925, to September, 1931, and after a buy signal indicated in March, 1942, no further action was dictated up to the end of 1953.

It is relatively easy to develop a formula with the Graham central value principle. The central value itself would, of course, be the median, and buying and selling points up and down the scale would indicate varying proportions of stocks and bonds, to avoid the all-or-nothing procedure outlined by Mr. Graham. Such a formula has been worked out, specifying a 50-50 stock-bond ratio at the median, with a 5 percent reduction in stocks at every 10 percent rise above the median and a 5 percent increase in stocks at every 10 percent drop below the median.[8] Maximum percentage of stocks is set at 65, and the minimum at 35. Excellent results were shown in the test, which covered the 1926-50 period. Value of the original portfolio nearly doubled, despite the fact that the Dow-Jones Industrial Average increased only about 40 percent.

Although Mr. Graham states the calculations of the central value from 1881 to 1936 "fall quite consistently within the actual price fluctuations during the period," the method has not worked so well recently. At this writing, the central value has for some years been considerably below the actual market level. This has been because stock prices have risen far faster than corporate earnings, and interest rates have also soared.

However, it would be foolish to predict dogmatically that the historical soundness of the theory will never hold true again. The spread between the central value and the Dow-Jones corrected itself in 1929, and it may do so again. At any rate, a formula based on the central value is sound in its basic principles, easy to operate, and—in the past—profitable.

THE BIRMINGHAM PLAN

The First National Bank in Birmingham, Alabama, has used a formula in the management of trust funds for over 15 years, and has over $100 million of funds under formula management.

The median is based on a continuing valuation of earning power of common stocks. Though the basis for the median is book value, the book value is adjusted according to earnings on invested capital, so that the foundation of the median turns out to be more a method of capitalized earnings. To get the median itself, an historical relationship is worked out between market price of a particular stock and its adjusted book value. The median for the Dow-Jones Average is based on separate valuations of each stock in the Average, divided by the current divisor.

The plan was worked out by C. P. Heartburg, trust officer of the bank. Mr. Heartburg expresses complete satisfaction with the formula, despite the fact that the median has tended in recent years to fall below the Dow-Jones Industrial Average. He explains this by saying that there is frequently a considerable deviation between the market and the median, but that the relationship has always tended to fall back into line. He cites as an example the 1937 market, when the average was 70 percent above the median, but later fell to bring the two into closer harmony. Since the mid-forties, the median has had an average annual increase of about 9 percent.

One difficulty with the plan is the disposition of new money added to various funds from time to time. The rules of the formula call for application of the halfway rule, which prohibits buying above the median. This creates a problem which has to be worked out in each individual case. Various proportions are used in different funds, of course, depending on the type of investor and his needs, and the bank's policy calls for using the plan as a guide, but not as an inflexible rule to be followed under all circumstances. The bank's clients, many of whom have had the formula thoroughly explained to them, are very happy with it—and with its results.

THE TEMPLETON, DOBBROW & VANCE FORMULA

A formula has been in use by Templeton, Dobbrow & Vance, Inc., Englewood, N. J., investment counselors, for more than 20 years. It cannot be used by other investors, because the exact nature of its computation has not been made public. The median is essentially a valuation of common stocks, based on such factors as book value, retained earnings and depreciation, plus other factors in the general economy, such as inflation.

The median, as calculated periodically, is a "normal" zone of varying width. In mid-1961, this "normal" zone stood at about 30 percent below the actual market, as measured by a stock average. However, such discrepancies do not worry the firm to any great extent. John Templeton, president, points out that the market has been above the median in about half the months since the formula was first used in 1938, and below the median in the other half, and that discrepancies, of whatever duration, have a habit of correcting themselves eventually.

Chart 4 shows the normal zone (shaded area) plotted

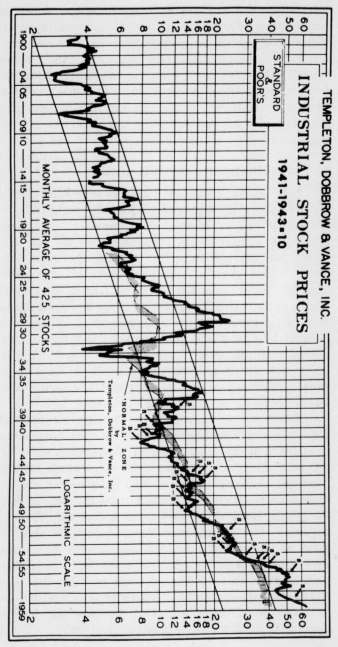

CHART 4: Performance of Templeton, Dobbrow & Vance periods are hypothetical.) Grey areas indicate range of formula. (Plan has been followed only from 1938. Prior median zone. (Supplied by Templeton, Dobbrow & Vance.)

against Standard & Poor's 425 Stock Average, drawn on logarithmic paper. The arrows marked "S" indicate points at which clients were advised to reduce stock holdings, and the arrows marked "B" are times at which they were advised to buy more stocks. (These arrows are shown only from 1938, when the formula was devised; the chart up to that time is of the hypothetical record.) As the chart shows, the formula pinpointed virtually every top and bottom in the market since it was first begun.

FIRM AND CLIENT AGREE

Most of the portfolios under the firm's management are managed according to indications given by the formula, although the precise manner in which the formula is used varies from account to account. When management of any new account is begun, the firm and the client agree on the levels above and below normal at which the proportions of stocks should be changed, and to what degree. Other features may also be included in the management philosophy of any particular account, such as a stipulation that the proportion of stocks not be changed until after a definite market trend shows signs of reversing itself (as shown by a moving average), or that at no point shall the proportion of stocks be reduced to zero or raised to 100 percent. The formula and its various modifications are described as "nonforecasting" programs.

Some portfolios managed by the firm are not under the formula but are—by agreement with the client—invested entirely in common stocks at all times. In others, proportions of stocks are determined by a constant-ratio plan (which the firm calls "constant percentage common stock programs"). The firm also offers to manage clients' investments on the basis of forecasting the general trend of the market, but it does not recommend this approach. Mr. Templeton remains enthusiastic about formula plans in general, and more than satisfied with the success of his own firm's formula. He emphasizes that an essential element in such plans is the avoidance of rigid and inflexible ideas. The TD&V formula has, in fact, undergone some revisions over the years as circumstances warranted, but none of them has apparently changed the basic principles involved.

THE GENSTEIN FORMULA

One of the newest—as well as one of the best—formulas was worked out by Edgar S. Genstein, a New Jersey industrialist (now retired), and made public for the first time in 1954 in his book, *Stock Market Profit Without Forecasting*.[9] Mr. Genstein devised his formula originally for his own use and as a result of research carried out over a number of years. The copyrighted data for the Genstein Formula are presented here by special permission of Mr. Genstein.

While the Genstein plan compares favorably with many of the more complicated formulas, the median itself is based on readily available data and can be computed by anyone who has a modicum of patience.

In contrast to Graham's central-value median (which is based on earnings), the Genstein current-dividend median uses the historical relationship between market prices and dividends as a standard by which current figures are measured. Three sets of data are required: (1) a 10-year record of the price range of the DJIA, (2) a 10-year record of dividend payments, and (3) the most recent annual dividends. (All these figures are published at irregular intervals in the "Market Laboratory" section of *Barron's*.)

The median is arrived at in the following steps:

1. Calculate the 10-year average of the quarterly high and low prices for the DJIA. This means adding the highs and lows for each quarter over the most recent 10-year period, and dividing by 80.

2. Calculate the 10-year average of annual dividends on the DJIA. This is done by adding all the quarterly dividend payments over the past 10 years and dividing by 40.

3. Divide (1) above by (2) above. This gives the average price-to-dividend ratio.

4. Calculate the dividends paid on the DJIA during the latest four quarters. This is simply a matter of adding the figures for the four most recent quarters.

5. Multiply the result obtained in (3) above by (4) above. This is the median.

Mr. Genstein stresses the importance of using the quarterly figures. This means that, if a plan were to be started in the third quarter of 1959, for example, the dividend and price-range figures will be used from 1950 through 1958, plus the last two quarters of 1949, and the first two of 1959. The median should be brought up to date every three months, as soon as the dividend figures become available, which is shortly after the end of each quarter.

What the plan amounts to is capitalizing current dividends at the rate which has been determined by the market over the past 10 years. Any changes in the market's opinions about how much should be paid for a dollar of dividend payments will be reflected in the median—not so soon as to cause violent fluctuations in the median, but soon enough to avoid rendering the plan useless while it catches up.

Table 8 shows the calculation of normal value, as well as the actual range of the Dow-Jones, from the beginning of 1948 to mid-1959, using figures supplied by Mr. Genstein. Chart 5 illustrates normal value plotted against the Dow-Jones actual ranges. As shown, the median detected the sharp undervaluation of market prices in reference to their true worth up to the middle of 1952, and again in mid-1953 and at the beginning of 1954. Since that time, the market has pulled gradually away from the median.

Buying and selling in the formula is operated according to a predetermined schedule of price levels set in terms of deviation from normal. Mr. Genstein's studies have indicated that "as far back as definitive figures are available, every major top has been characterized by prices that were at least 1.40 times the computed normal, while every major bottom has been characterized by prices that were at least as low as normal divided by 1.40." [10] Mr. Genstein assumes that when price deviations from normal are greater than these 1.40 levels, the market is in a major selling or buying zone. Schedules are set up for future fluctuations of prices to 1.45-1.60 times normal, and normal divided by 1.45-1.60, as shown in Table 9, reproduced from Mr. Genstein's book. [11] Four plans are set up, referred to in the table as A, B, C and D, going from the most to the least aggressive. The most conservative plan holds to minimum percentages for stocks that are above those prescribed for the less conservative plans. (Mr. Genstein suggests that "Plan B is considered

TABLE 8

THE GENSTEIN FORMULA, 1948-59*

YEAR & QUARTER	10-YEAR MOVING AVERAGES PRICES	DIVS.	10-YR. P/D NORMAL RATIO	DJIA DIVS. LATEST 12 MOS.	NORMAL VALUE DJIA	RANGE ACTUAL DJIA
1948-1	146.7 ÷	6.91 =	21.2 ×	9.46 =	201	165-181
2	148.4	7.06	21.0	9.83	206	177-193
3	149.5	7.19	20.8	10.16	211	176-192
4	150.3	7.49	20.1	11.50	231	171-191
1949-1	151.1	7.65	19.8	11.93	236	171-182
2	152.1	7.79	19.5	12.19	238	162-177
3	152.9	7.88	19.4	12.09	235	168-183
4	153.9	8.16	18.9	12.79	242	182-200
1950-1	155.3	8.32	18.7	13.21	247	197-211
2	157.4	8.45	18.6	13.34	248	206-228
3	159.5	8.68	18.4	14.89	274	197-227
4	161.9	9.07	17.8	16.13	287	222-235
1951-1	164.9	9.30	17.7	17.00	301	239-256
2	168.2	9.46	17.8	17.50	311	243-263
3	171.6	9.67	17.7	17.35	307	241-276
4	175.3	9.94	17.6	16.34	288	256-276
1952-1	179.3	10.16	17.6	16.16	284	258-275
2	183.4	10.37	17.7	16.28	288	256-274
3	187.6	10.58	17.7	16.11	285	268-280
4	191.7	10.85	17.7	15.48	274	263-292
1953-1	195.7	11.08	17.7	15.54	275	280-294
2	199.0	11.32	17.6	15.89	280	263-280
3	202.2	11.53	17.5	15.87	278	255-277
4	205.6	11.83	17.4	16.11	280	264-284
1954-1	209.5	12.09	17.3	16.38	283	280-304
2	214.0	12.32	17.4	16.35	284	304-337
3	219.0	12.55	17.5	16.57	289	334-364
4	224.8	12.92	17.4	17.47	304	352-404
1955-1	231.0	13.27	17.4	18.39	320	388-420
2	237.7	13.52	17.6	18.71	329	413-451
3	245.1	13.80	17.8	19.21	341	449-487
4	251.9	14.41	17.5	21.58	377	439-488
1956-1	259.2	14.75	17.57	21.63	380	462-513
2	266.4	15.08	17.67	22.37	395	469-521
3	274.2	15.39	17.82	22.95	409	475-521
4	282.1	15.96	17.68	22.99	406	466-499
1957-1	289.6	16.27	17.80	22.98	409	455-499
2	297.7	16.53	18.01	22.79	410	475-513
3	305.4	16.81	18.17	22.87	416	456-521
4	311.9	17.20	18.13	21.61	392	420-466
1958-1	318.8	17.48	18.24	21.57	393	437-459
2	325.7	17.68	18.42	21.40	394	440-479
3	333.7	17.90	18.64	21.08	393	477-532
4	343.1	18.05	19.01	20.00	380	531-584
1959-1	353.6	18.28	19.34	19.93	385	574-615
2	364.9	18.45	19.78	19.90	394	603-644

*Figures supplied and copyrighted by Edgar S. Genstein.

suitable for average requirements.") Added to the table are the actual Dow-Jones Industrial price levels that correspond to the indicated deviations from normal value, as computed for June 30, 1959.

The formula calls for re-examination of the account quarterly, when new figures become available. Adjustments in the portfolio—if required—are made at that time. Mr. Genstein suggests the use of "delaying action," in which stocks bought far below the median are held until stock prices have advanced somewhat above it, in order to profit more fully from a sustained price rise. Similarly, "stocks sold substantially above the median are not replaced until prices have declined to a point well below the median." The halfway rule is observed, which prevents any purchases of stocks above the median, or any sales below.[12]

Publication of Mr. Genstein's book in 1954 aroused a great deal of interest among students of formula methods as well as among investors—both individuals and institutions. Demand was

TABLE 9

ALTERNATE PLANS FOR THE GENSTEIN FORMULA*

PRICE LEVEL	DJIA LEVELS FOR 6/30/59	PERCENTAGE OF FUND TO BE HELD IN STOCKS			
		PLAN A	PLAN B	PLAN C	PLAN D
1.60 × Normal	630			10	25
1.55 × Normal	611		10	15	
1.50 × Normal	591		15	20	30
1.45 × Normal	571	10	20	25	
1.40 × Normal	552	20	25	30	35
1.35 × Normal	532	30	30	35	
1.30 × Normal	512	40	35	40	40
1.25 × Normal	493	50	40	45	
1.20 × Normal	473		45	50	45
1.15 × Normal	453		50		
1.10 × Normal	433				50
Normal	394	50	50	50	50
Normal ÷ 1.10	358				50
Normal ÷ 1.15	343		50		
Normal ÷ 1.20	328		55	50	55
Normal ÷ 1.25	315	50	60	55	
Normal ÷ 1.30	303	60	65	60	60
Normal ÷ 1.35	292	70	70	65	
Normal ÷ 1.40	281	80	75	70	65
Normal ÷ 1.45	272	90	80	75	
Normal ÷ 1.50	263		85	80	70
Normal ÷ 1.55	254		90	85	
Normal ÷ 1.60	246			90	75

*Reproduced from "Stock Market Profit Without Forecasting," by Edgar S. Genstein, with figures for Dow-Jones Industrial Average for June 30, 1959, added.

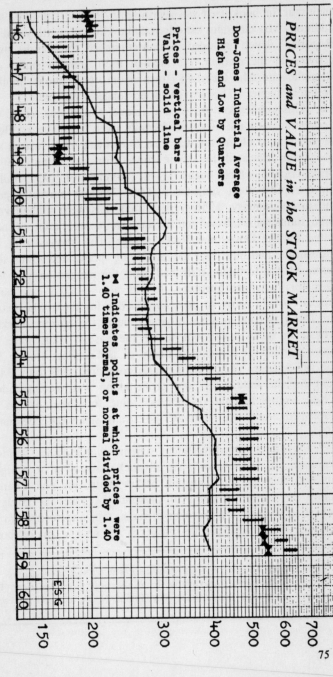

PRICES and VALUE in the STOCK MARKET

Dow-Jones Industrial Average
High and Low by Quarters

Prices - vertical bars
Value - solid line

M Indicates points at which prices were
1.40 times normal, or normal divided by 1.40

CHART 5: Genstein current-dividend median, plotted against   Genstein's "Supplementary Quarterly Reports," July, 1959.)
the Dow-Jones Industrial Average, 1946-59. (From Edgar S.

such that the book itself was reprinted in 1956, 1958 and 1961. In addition, Mr. Genstein established the "Supplementary Quarterly Reports," which included computations of the figures used in arriving at the median, the median itself, current status of the formula, and Mr. Genstein's own acute observations on the investment scene. (This service is no longer available.)

This publication provided a unique, continuous record of the performance of the Genstein formula over recent years. Because of observance of the halfway rule, no buying of industrial stocks has been indicated for some time. However, after the sharp price decline which began in the summer of 1957, rails fell more rapidly than industrials. Mr. Genstein correctly pointed out in his January, 1958, report, that rails were a "better value than industrials," based on a separate computation of normal value for the Dow-Jones Rail Average. This showed that, while industrials had not reached a buying point according to the terms of the formula, rails had, and the suggestion was to use rails for switching purposes. It was also pointed out that rail stocks "should prove to be a good hedge for those who fear that the DJIA will not reach a buying zone in the current market"—which, in fact, turned out to be the case.[13] Rails were again recommended in subsequent issues of the service. During 1958, the rail average gained 63 percent, compared with only 34 percent for the industrials, and profit-taking was recommended in 1959. Complete data on normal value for the rails has been published along with that on industrials since the beginning of 1958.

Obviously, any investment scheme that includes bonds will compare unfavorably with an all-stock position in a straight-up market. But, as Mr. Genstein makes plain, his plan "can certainly be depended upon to prevent purchases at levels that subsequently prove to be near a major top, and to prevent sales at levels that subsequently prove to be near a major bottom.

The revised edition of *Stock Market Profit without Forecasting*, by Edgar S. Genstein, is available from the publisher, American Research Council, 2 East Avenue, Larchmont, N. Y., at $3.50 per copy.

That in itself—even if the plan accomplishes nothing more—is sufficient reason for its existence." [14]

A study of the formula's operation from September, 1938, to September, 1957 (using the schedule specified in Plan A), showed an increase of a $100,000 fund to $325,000. At the beginning of the plan, the account was 50 percent in stocks. In contrast, a $100,000 "buy and hold" fund, also 50 percent in stocks at the beginning, increased in value only to' $213,000. In addition to the more rapid appreciation of the formula-managed fund, it held only 23 percent of its total value in stocks at the end, compared with a 77 percent position for the "buy and hold" fund. Thus the formula-managed account was in a much stronger position to withstand a bear market. [15]

An important fact to note is that the Genstein median does not attempt to tell the market how it should act. If the stock market is in a "new era," in which prices are due to fluctuate at much higher levels than ever before—as is sometimes suggested [16]—the Genstein median will reflect the fact, but not until it is a firmly established fact. Meanwhile, it will continue to provide protection against any disastrous decline which could ensue in the meantime, and will put the investor in a good position to profit from wide market swings.

THE TOMLINSON "COMPROMISE" PLAN

One formula described by Miss Tomlinson combines the minimum-forecasting feature of constant-ratio plans with the advantages of variable-ratio plans. [17] On the one hand, this improves the constant-ratio principle to the extent that greater profits can be gained in bull markets and greater protection in bear periods than is possible with a constant ratio. On the other hand it prevents the investor from reducing stocks to a negligible figure during extended advances, as is sometimes the case with variable ratios.

The plan is operated like a variable-ratio formula, but instead of varying the stock portion between extremely low and extremely high percentages, as is usually done, it is to be adjusted only between 40 and 60 percent. Miss Tomlinson points out that the choice of a median is of relatively small importance,

77

since the profitability of the method does not depend on it to so great an extent as in other formulas. She suggests that any workable median can be used, and herself uses the Graham central value in a test. In case the median is totally wrong, the worst that can happen is that the investor will be operating a constant-ratio plan, with either 40 percent or 60 percent of his account in stocks. The halfway rule is not to be observed, so that portfolio adjustments can be made at any time. The action points are placed at 20 percent intervals above the median, and at 16⅔ percent intervals below, which gives the same amount of point change.

In comparisons worked out with a normal constant ratio and a "buy and hold" account, Miss Tomlinson shows a clear superiority of the "compromise plan" over both.

This formula is an extremely practical one, requiring little in the way of involved calculations, but at the same time profitable and suitable to the average investor. In late 1959, the median (assuming the central value method were used) would be at about half the actual Dow-Jones Average, and the market would long ago have indicated a minimum position in stocks. But since the minimum is 40 percent, the investor would still be able to profit somewhat from further rises in the market, and would be protected to a considerable degree from a decline.

SIX

SHOULD YOU USE A FORMULA?

It has been emphasized that the main vogue for formulas began in the late thirties, and was primarily a reaction to the market declines of 1929-32 and 1937-38. Naturally, the market analysts who first worked with formulas were more interested in building protection against declines than profiting from advances, and they understandably assumed that the severity of future drops in market prices would match these two earlier periods.

It is almost impossible to resist the temptation to forecast stock prices, and it is difficult for a formula investigator to know at any particular time whether he is making a forecast on the basis of available facts or whether he is allowing his optimism or pessimism of the moment to dominate his efforts. In 1949, for example, one investigator wrote about the original Keystone plan—whose weakness has turned out to be too low a secular growth rate—"more recent stock-price fluctuations gives us some cause to question the assumption that the trend will be as strongly upward in the future as it appears to have been over the entire period from 1897 to 1946."[1] If this commentator had been writing either three years earlier or three years later, it is doubtful that he would have made such a criticism.[1]

As we have seen, a number of bank trust departments and investment counselors use formulas, but it is likely that many more use them as a guide than are willing to publicize the fact. One trust officer has said he doubted if very many trust departments used formulas, because "they wouldn't want to admit their judgment was that bad." One large investment advisory organization has spent a great deal of effort drawing up a median based on a wide range of economic and market data, but has consistently refused to make the fact public, since it doesn't want to be identified with formulas, even though it uses this median on some portfolios it manages, with the clients' approval.

A large number of investors, particularly institutions, still use formulas and are quite happy with them. Although some of the pioneering endowment funds, such as those of Yale, Vassar and Oberlin, have given them up, many others, including those of Syracuse and Kenyon, still use formulas and are satisfied with the results.

ARE FORMULAS WORTH USING?

Whether or not any particular investor should use a formula is, of course, a matter of individual judgment. Some formulas, such as the Genstein Plan, require a fair amount of calculation, and many people are unwilling to discipline themselves to set aside time to manage their investments.

At the high points of big bull markets, many investors are ready to scoff at formulas. It is true that any portfolio containing bonds is at a disadvantage during bull markets, but how many individual portfolios perform as well as the Dow-Jones during a bull market? Besides, who is to predict that the market will always be one big bull market after another? A formula is powerless to take maximum advantage of a straight-up price rise, but the more normal pattern of stock prices is to undergo frequent periods of decline also. The "ideal formula timing plan," as summed up by one authority "is not that which secures the greatest gain for a given assumed pattern of security-price fluctuations but one which achieves the greatest gain for a degree of risk appropriate to the circumstances of the investor." [2]

Undoubtedly, the prestige of formula investing is at its lowest ebb during periods of steadily rising prices, but after every decline a new revival of interest occurs, simultaneous with the discovery by many investors that they are not the analytical geniuses they had previously thought themselves to be. In 1949, for example, formula investing had proved itself superior to the average investor's judgment, and *Business Week* reported: "Despite the steep hills and valleys on market price charts, formula-investing during the past two decades would have produced far better results than those achieved by most individual money managers." [3]

SECURITY SELECTION

One subject that has not been touched on so far is the question of how to select the common stocks for a formula-managed portfolio. In the examples examined in this book, one or another of the popular stock averages has been used to indicate movement of the stock portion of the account. Obviously, investors do not buy stock averages.

Most commentators on formula investing suggest that investors buy stocks of above-average volatility. This would include most of the relatively high quality "growth stocks." It is not necessary to concentrate only on such stocks, however. What is important is to buy only those stocks which are actively traded, of good quality, and subject to at least average fluctuation.

As noted previously, there is no necessity for the investor to give up his prerogative of selecting the stocks he feels suit his requirements best. Whether he concentrates on conservative blue-chip stocks, growth stocks or wildly speculative issues, he can get the same benefits from a formula. The purpose of a formula—even if the investor using it does not always follow its dictates with precision—is to provide a touchstone for adjusting one's portfolio against probable market moves and maintaining a strong financial position under all circumstances. And this purpose will be fulfilled no matter what stocks the investor selects.

In speaking of the indications given by formulas, it is not intended that the investor necessarily retain exactly the same stocks at all times, even though the formula specifies that a certain proportion of stocks be held. The formula investor should pay careful attention to his portfolio and switch his stocks around somewhat as their outlooks change.

HOW TO BUILD YOUR OWN FORMULA

The investor who concludes that he might profit by using a formula is, naturally, faced with the problem of what type he wants to use, and exactly what rules he is going to set up for himself. A basic consideration, of course, is the amount of risk he is willing to assume.

The element of risk is present in all investment schemes, and it is the purpose of a formula to minimize it, while working toward some growth of capital. The amount of risk the investor wants to build into his formula is up to him—the more risk the greater the profit possibilities. The constant-ratio plans examined earlier assumed a 50-50 stock-bond relationship, but an investor willing to take on more risk would be perfectly justified in setting the stock percentage substantially higher—at 80 percent, say.

Although, as discussed in detail earlier, there is no "best" formula that will suit all investors, the two which are widely used, practical, easy to operate and profitable over periods of time are *dollar averaging* and the *constant-ratio* plan. Most investors can undoubtedly profit by using one or another of these, adjusting them to suit individual needs. As noted previously, the two can quite easily be combined to take advantage of the merits of each. If it were possible to predict what type of market is in the cards for next year, it would be easy to construct exactly the right formula—but then it would be even easier and more profitable to throw out formulas altogether.

OTHER FACTORS INFLUENTIAL

Aside from the question of risk, convenience and psychological satisfaction also must influence the choice of a formula. For example, an investor who finds even the relatively simple mathematics involved in the Graham or Genstein intrinsic-value plans irksome would be foolish to try to follow such a system. And the investor who has little faith in the infallibility of the Keystone channels would undoubtedly not for long follow one of them even if he started. The formula must "feel" right; the investor must be convinced of the value of the formula, so that he will not be tempted to discard it when it happens to be performing poorly.

The writer has not attempted to present every formula ever invented. The formulas described are felt to offer a representative sampling of the most practical or widely publicized types to enable the investor to select whatever features he may prefer. There are numerous possibilities for other plans. A good source of future formula methods might well be in market "timing" techniques such as the "confidence index," one or another of the breadth indexes or advance-decline indicators, or the strength measurements issued by Lowry's Reports. These technical approaches to the market could undoubtedly be adapted easily to the formula principle. A formula based on current stock yields would probably have given good results over past years.

It is possible that a good formula could be built around the loan-deposit ratios of commercial banks, the underlying assumption being that the Federal Reserve Board—which influences this ratio by its actions in the money market—is a major influence on the stock market. Although the relationship of business cycles to stock market cycles was distant during the war and postwar years, it may be that a formula based on business indicators might again be profitable in the future. All these areas, of course, would require detailed investigation, but the important point is that the reader need not feel restricted to the formulas that have been devised in the past.

In order to show how an original formula may be constructed with little trouble, this writer has devised and tested a modification of the constant ratio formula, based on odd lot indexes, that would have given adequate results over a number of years. Like the "compromise plan" described on page 77, it is simply the constant ratio plan with an added feature, based on odd lot trading, to improve results.

As used by specialists in the study of odd lot statistics, the significance of these extends far beyond that indicated by the use made of them in this formula.[1] For the present purpose, it will be sufficient to point out that studies conducted by Garfield A. Drew have shown that enthusiasm of odd lot investors for stocks at certain periods may signal danger in the market, while an indifferent or bearish attitude may signal a market low point. Each day, the number of shares bought and sold in odd lots on the New York Stock Exchange during the preceding trading day are released by the Exchange and published in leading newspapers. The index used in this formula is the Odd Lot Balance Index originated by Garfield A. Drew and regularly published by Drew Investment Associates of Boston. It is a three-month moving average of the ratio of odd lot sales to purchases, multiplied by 100. An index, for example, shows that sales exactly equalled purchases; a figure of 90 means that sales were 90 percent of purchases. The higher the index goes, the more stock odd lot investors are selling relative to their purchases, and the

TABLE 10

DATE	MOODY'S 125 STOCKS	ODD-LOT BALANCE INDEX	STOCK-BOND RATIO CALLED FOR	BEFORE ACTION	
				STOCKS	BONDS
Jan., 1944	34.61	89.8	50-50		
July	37.22	92.1	75-25	$10,753	$10,000
Jan., 1945	39.35	93.6	75-25	16,620	5,032
July	42.13	87.1	50-50	17,387	5,413
Jan., 1946	52.31	80.0	50-50	14,156	11,400
July	52.67	80.5	50-50	12,866	12,778
Jan., 1947	46.86	85.9	50-50	11,408	12,822
July	47.88	94.3	75-25	12,379	12,115
Jan., 1948	45.42	90.0	75-25	17,427	6,123
July	48.60	99.9	75-25	18,899	5,888
Jan., 1949	46.36	82.6	50-50	17,733	6,197
July	46.01	94.4	75-25	11,874	11,965
Jan., 1950	52.58	106.8	75-25	20,430	5,960
July	56.43	96.9	75-25	21,241	6,598
Jan., 1951	68.21	93.6	75-25	25,238	6,960
July	71.28	79.5	50-50	25,234	8,050
Jan., 1952	75.09	79.4	50-50	17,531	16,642
July	78.01	84.9	50-50	17,751	17,087
Jan., 1953	80.37	92.4	75-25	17,946	17,419
July	76.24	84.1	50-50	25,159	8,841
Jan., 1954	81.37	100.2	75-25	18,144	17,000
July	98.49	98.4	75-25	31,903	8,786
Jan., 1955	116.83	102.4	75-25	36,198	10,172
July	137.85	84.3	50-50	41,035	11,593
Jan., 1956	140.11	83.9	50-50	26,746	26,314
July	158.98	81.1	50-50	30,102	26,530
Jan., 1957	142.80	73.7	50-50	25,434	28,316
July	157.66	83.4	50-50	29,671	26,875
Jan., 1958	133.06	81.1	50-50	23,861	28,273
July	151.57	98.1	75-25	29,579	26,067
Dec., 1958	177.75	...	....	....	....

lower it goes, the more stock they are buying relative to their sales. For this formula, the significance of the figures is that when odd lotters are heavy sellers, it is time to increase stock holdings, and when they are buying heavily, it is time to sell some stocks.

As drawn up, the formula is a 50-50 stock-bond constant ratio, with the proviso that when the Odd Lot Balance Index

MODIFIED CONSTANT RATIO TEST, 1944-58

ACTION			AFTER ACTION STOCKS	BONDS	VALUE OF ACCOUNT	DATE
Begin Plan			$10,000	$10,000	$20,000	Jan., 1944
Buy	$4,967	stocks	15,720	5,032	20,752	July
Sell	$380	stocks	16,239	5,413	21,652	Jan., 1945
Sell	$5,987	stocks	11,400	11,400	22,800	July
Sell	$1,378	stocks	12,778	12,778	22,556	Jan., 1946
Sell	$44	stocks	12,822	12,822	25,644	July
Buy	$707	stocks	12,115	12,115	24,230	Jan., 1947
Buy	$5,992	stocks	18,371	6,123	24,494	July
Buy	$235	stocks	17,662	5,888	23,550	Jan., 1948
Sell	$309	stocks	18,590	6,197	24,787	July
Sell	$5,768	stocks	11,965	11,965	23,930	Jan., 1949
Buy	$6,004	stocks	17,879	5,960	23,839	July
Sell	$638	stocks	19,792	6,598	26,390	Jan., 1950
Sell	$362	stocks	20,879	6,960	27,839	July
Sell	$1,090	stocks	24,148	8,050	32,198	Jan., 1951
Sell	$8,592	stocks	16,642	16,642	33,284	July
Sell	$444	stocks	17,087	17,087	34,174	Jan., 1952
Sell	$332	stocks	17,419	17,419	34,838	July
Buy	$8,577	stocks	26,523	8,841	35,365	Jan., 1953
Sell	$8,159	stocks	17,000	17,000	34,000	July
Buy	$8,214	stocks	26,358	8,786	35,144	Jan., 1954
Sell	$1,386	stocks	30,517	10,172	40,689	July
Sell	$1,420	stocks	34,778	11,593	46,370	Jan., 1955
Sell	$14,721	stocks	26,314	26,314	52,628	July
Sell	$216	stocks	26,530	26,530	53,060	Jan., 1956
Sell	$1,786	stocks	28,316	28,316	56,632	July
Buy	$1,441	stocks	26,875	26,875	53,750	Jan., 1957
Sell	$1,398	stocks	28,273	28,273	56,546	July
Buy	$2,206	stocks	26,067	26,067	52,134	Jan., 1958
Buy	$12,155	stocks	41,734	13,912	55,646	July
	....		....	....	62,853	Dec., 1958

rises above 90, the stock portion of the account is raised to
75 percent, and the bond portion accordingly reduced to 25 percent. The account is reviewed every six months, and changes
made as indicated. If no change in the stock-bond relationship
is dictated, then the account is readjusted to the previous percentages. (Other percentages could be adopted—a 40 percent
stock ratio when the Index is below 90, for example, and 90 percent

when it is above. Also, the account could be adjusted whenever a certain specified shift had occurred in the market instead of at six-month intervals, although this would not have affected final results to any great degree.)

The Odd Lot Balance Index is shown graphically in Chart 6, plotted with Moody's 125-stock index for the 15-year period 1944-58. The shaded areas indicate the points when the Odd Lot Balance Index rose above 90. Table 7 shows the action carried out during the 15-year test period, and the results. Starting with a portfolio of $20,000, the formula managed to more than triple this original figure by the end of the period, the final value of the portfolio being $62,853. These results were, during this period, inferior to the increase in the stock average itself, which rose fivefold, but the formula did allow some growth of capital, while remaining essentially conservative and thus offering considerable protection during market declines.

It will be seen that there were six periods during which an increased percentage of stocks was called for. In four of these, the stock average was significantly higher at the ends of the periods than at the beginning, and in two, small declines were posted. Inasmuch as the declines were in neither case more than 5 percent, and the advances ranged from 12 to 67 percent, it can be fairly concluded that the modification of the plan was profitable. It must be emphasized that the formula incorporates a greatly simplified use of the odd lot figures, and does not attempt to reduce stocks just before a decline, or to increase them right at the bottom (although in some instances it did just that). It dictated a cutback in stocks nearly a year before the high of 1946 was reached, for example, and, after increasing stocks at almost the exact bottom in 1949, reduced again in mid-1951, only to buy back at a higher level in 1954. It will be noted, however, that it did enable the investor *to profit from the larger part of every major advance during the 15-year period*, and protected him from loss during weak and aimless price trends. In addition, satisfactory appreciation was registered in the account.

In one month—March, 1953—the Odd Lot Balance Index dipped briefly below 90 to 89.2, only to rise again the next month to above 90. If, instead of the six-month interval specified for readjustments in this formula, an investor had changed his

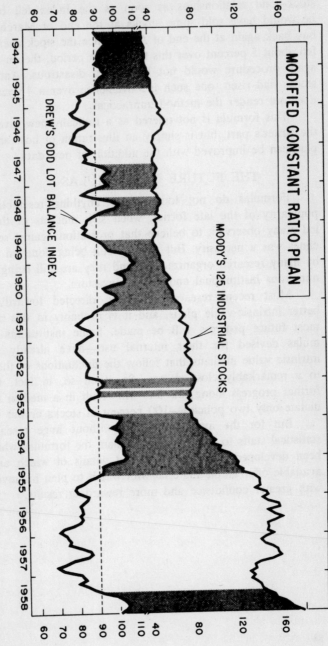

MODIFIED CONSTANT RATIO PLAN

DREW'S ODD LOT BALANCE INDEX

MOODY'S 125 INDUSTRIAL STOCKS

CHART 6: Modified constant-ratio plan, using the odd-lot balance index as a guide. Grey areas indicate periods during which odd-lot index is above 90, when stock portion of account may be increased. (Odd-lot balance index figures supplied by Drew Investment Associates, Inc.)

87

stock-bond relationships as soon as the Index fell below 90, he would have sold some stocks at the end of March, only to buy back again at the end of April. Since the stock average itself fell about 5 percent over this two-month period, the on-again-off-again procedure would not have been disastrous. And even if stocks had risen, one such inconvenience over a 15-year period does not render the method impractical.

This formula is not offered as a radically new invention on the writer's part, but is simply an illustration of how an existing plan can be improved with the addition of new data.

THE FUTURE OF FORMULAS

Formulas do not today enjoy anything resembling their popularity of the late forties, when sick markets of the period led many observers to believe that protection against severe declines was a necessity. But work is still being done on formulas by many research organizations, and they are still being used by numerous institutional and private investors.

Most recent research has been directed toward devising better intrinsic-value plans, and it is probably in this area that most future progress will be made. Some institutions—in formulas devised for their internal use—have already achieved intrinsic value medians that follow the fluctuations of the market to a remarkably close degree. So much so, in fact, that any further progress along this line will result in a median that will dictate only two policies—100 percent in stocks or out of them.

But for the average investor without huge research and statistical staffs to work out his median, the formulas which have been developed over the years and details of which are freely available offer ample material with which to plan his investments with greater confidence and more rewarding results.

NOTES and
SELECTED BIBLIOGRAPHY

Notes

CHAPTER 1

[1] "Wall Streeters Who Were Right," *Fortune*, May, 1958, p. 110.

[2] Lawrence Tighe, in an address before the American Bankers Association, February, 1940, quoted in H. G. Carpenter, *Investment Timing by Formula Plans*, New York, Harper & Bros., 1943, p. 14.

[3] Alfred Cowles, "Stock Market Forecasting," *Econometrica*, July-October, 1944, pp 206-14. An earlier study along the same lines, entitled "Can Stock Market Forecasters Forecast?" appeared in the same periodical in July, 1933, pp. 309-324.

[4] Paul Francis Wendt, *The Classification and Financial Experience of the Customers of a Typical New York Stock Exchange Firm from 1933 to 1938*, Ann Arbor, Mich., Edwards Bros., Inc., 1941. This study was summarized in *Barron's*. March 16 and March 30. 1942. under the title "Do Wall Street's Customers Win or Lose?"

[5] Robert Warren, "Formula Plan Investing," *Harvard Business Review*, January-February, 1953, pp. 57-70.

[6] O. K. Burrell, *An Experiment in Speculative Behavior*, Eugene, Ore., Bureau of Business Research, University of Oregon, 1950.

[7] Donald I. Rogers, "Why People Really Buy Stocks," *New York Herald Tribune*, June 12, 1959, section 3, page 4.

[8] Carpenter, op. cit., p. 57.

[9] Lucile Tomlinson, *Practical Formulas for Successful Investing*, New York, Wilfred Funk, 1953, p. 213.

CHAPTER 2

[1] Neil Maxwell, "Public Portfolios," *The Wall Street Journal*, May 29, 1959, p. 1.

[2] "Just How Good Are Common Stocks?" New York Stock Exchange, 1956.

[3] Roger Bridwell, "Magic Formula? Dollar Averaging Sometimes Can Lead to Losses," *Barron's*, February 3, 1958, pp. 38-39.

[4] "Way to Recoup Stock Losses," *Business Week*, March 15, 1958, pp. 135-138.

[5] Tomlinson, *op. cit.*, p. 58.

[6] "Way to Recoup Stock Losses," *Business Week*, March 15, 1958, pp. 135-138.

[7] Martin Mayer, *Wall Street: Men and Money*, New York, Harper & Bros., 1955, pp. 97-99.

CHAPTER 3

[1] C. Sidney Cottle and W. Tate Whitman, *Investment Timing: the Formula Plan Approach*, New York, McGraw-Hill Book Co., 1953, p. 158.

CHAPTER 4

[1] Cottle and Whitman, *op. cit.*, p. 33.

[2] Tomlinson, *op. cit.*, p. 148.

[3] Cottle and Whitman, *op. cit.*, pp. 33-36.

[4] Ezra Solomon, "Are Formula Plans What They Seem to Be?" *Journal of Business*, April, 1948, pp. 92-97.

[5] S. C. Fleming, "Investment Prescription—Formula Plan Theory," *Barron's*, March 17, 1952, p. 13.

CHAPTER 5

[1] Carpenter, *op. cit.*, p. 43.

[2] "Colleges and Equities," *Barron's*, April 6, 1959, p. 9.

[3] Warren, *op. cit.*

[4] Tomlinson, *op. cit.*, pp. 171-175.

[5] A full explanation of this plan is given in Sherman F. Feyler, *Income Growth with Security*, New York, Macmillan, 1958, pp. 87-92.

[6] Feyler, *op. cit.*, pp. 75-79.

[7] Benjamin Graham, *The Intelligent Investor*, New York, Harper & Bros., 1954, pp. 259-264.

[8] Cottle and Whitman, *op. cit.*, pp. 109-117.

[9] Edgar S. Genstein, *Stock Market Profit Without Forecasting*, American Research Council, 2 East Avenue, Larchmont, N. Y., 1954-56, $3.50.

[10] *Ibid.*, p. 41.

[11] *Ibid.*, p. 38.

[12] *Ibid.*, p. 44.

[13] "Supplementary Quarterly Reports," Investment Research Press, 45 University Court, South Orange, N. J., January, 1958.

[14] Genstein, *op. cit.*, p. 50.

[15] "Supplementary Quarterly Reports," October, 1957.

[16] Gilbert Burck, "A New Kind of Stock Market," Fortune, March, 1959, p. 120.

[17] Tomlinson, *op. cit.*, pp. 232-238.

CHAPTER 6

[1] Marshall D. Ketchum, "Adjustment for the Secular Trend of Stock Prices in Formula Timing Plans," Journal of Business, Jan. 1949, p. 29.

[2] J. Fred Weston, "Some Theoretical Aspects of Formula Timing Plans," Journal of Business, October 1949, pp. 49-70.

[3] "Beating the Swings by Formula," *Business Week*, November 5, 1949, pp. 63-66.

[4] An excellent description of the odd lot technique is included in Garfield Drew, *New Methods for Profit in the Stock Market*, Boston, The Metcalf Press, 1955, pp. 193-234. A briefer explanation is presented in "Are Market Turns Predictable?" *Forbes*, July 15, 1958, pp. 13-16.

Selected Bibliography on Formula Investing

BOOKS

Carpenter. H. G., *Investment Timing by Formula Plans*, New York, Harper & Bros., 1943.

Cottle, C. Sidney, and Whitman, W. Tate, *Investment Timing: The Formula Plan Approach*, New York, McGraw-Hill Book Co., 1953.

Drew, Garfield A., *New Methods for Profit in the Stock Market*, Boston, The Metcalf Press, 1955, pp. 98-141.

Feyler, Sherman F., *Income Growth with Security*, New York, Macmillan, 1958.

Genstein, Edgar S., *Stock Market Profit without Forecasting*, Larchmont, N. Y., American Research Council, 1953. Revised edition 1956.

Tomlinson, Lucile, *Practical Formulas for Successful Investing*, New York, Wilfred Funk, 1953.

ARTICLES

Bridwell, Roger, "Magic Formula? Dollar Averaging Sometimes Can Lead to Losses," *Barron's*, February 3, 1958, p. 38-39.

Business Week, "Beating the Swings by Formula," November 5, 1949, pp. 63-64.

———"Way to Recoup Stock Losses," March 15, 1958, pp. 135-138.

Cottle, C. Sidney, "Factors to Be Considered in Appraising Formula Plans," *Southern Economic Journal*, July, 1949, pp. 62-69.

Cottle, C. Sidney, and Whitman, W. Tate, "Formula Plans and the Institutional Investor," *Harvard Business Review*, July, 1950, pp. 84-96.

———"Testing Formula Plans," *Commercial and Financial Chronicle*, January 4, 1951, p. 65.

———"Testing Formula Plans," *Journal of Finance*, June, 1951, pp. 220-229.

Financial World, "Formula Plans as Investment Tools," February 26, 1958, p. 7.

———"Taking the Guess Out of Investing," February 19, 1958, pp. 4-5.

Fleming, S. C., "Investment Prescription—Formula Plan Theory," *Barron's*, March 17, 1952, p. 13.

Jones, A. W., "Fashions in Forecasting," *Fortune*, March, 1949, pp. 88-97.

Ketchum, Marshall D., "Adjustment for the Secular Trend of Stock Prices in Formula Timing Plans," *Journal of Business*, January, 1948, pp. 29-49.

———"Can Life Insurance Companies Use Formula Plans?" *Journal of Business*, January, 1949, pp. 30-49.

Solomon, Ezra, "Are Formula Plans What They Seem to Be?" *Journal of Business,* April, 1948, pp. 92-97.

Szatrowski, Zenon, "Objective Investment Formula Plan," *Commercial and Financial Chronicle,* May 1, 1952, p. 1819.

———"Statistical Approach to Formula Planning," *The Analysts Journal,* May, 1955, pp. 65-69.

Tomlinson, Lucile, "Formulas Tested—Scientific Investment Plans Have Survived the Bull Market," *Barron's,* October 10, 1955, pp. 5-6.

Warren, Robert, "Formula Plan Investing," *Harvard Business Review,* January-February, 1953, pp. 57-70.

Weston, J. Fred, "Some Theoretical Aspects of Formula Timing Plans," *Journal of Business,* October, 1949, pp. 49-70.

Zukoski, "Ten Years of Investment under Formula Timing Plans," *Commercial and Financial Chronicle,* January 4, 1952, p. 657.

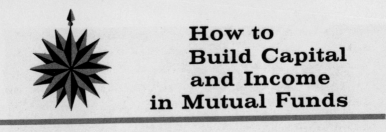

How to Build Capital and Income in Mutual Funds

How this book can help you:

Millions of Americans now own and are buying shares of mutual funds, because these have proved themselves to be versatile, convenient and valuable investments. You can use mutual funds for a wide range of goals — to build for your retirement, to start a fund for your children's education or for any other financial objective, to put your extra money to work for you, or to hedge against inflation. If you like constructive, stable investments, there are mutual funds for you. If you prefer a daring, more speculative approach — with opportunities for greater gain but greater risk, you can also find mutual funds to suit you. Whatever your income, age, family situation, objectives or emotional make-up, chances are there is a mutual fund that fits your requirements.

This concise, practical treatment gives you the background to make up your own mind, to expand your range of choice and reduce your dependence on the salesman. Here you can see what mutual funds are and how they operate, what to look for in a fund, different methods of buying funds, tips on how to choose the best one for you, exactly what costs are involved and methods of reducing these costs, how a fund may help you reduce your tax burden, where to go to buy a mutual fund, and what questions you should ask the fund's representatives.

Included are valuable checklists showing results of dollar averaging in mutual funds, funds with leverage or other speculative features, funds offering above-average yields, management results of the funds, funds with no sales charge or very low charges, funds with low expense ratio —and a complete directory of funds, addresses, sales charges and other data.

The author, David Jenkins, has no interest in any specific fund, nor any axe to grind on the subject of mutual funds. He is an experienced financial writer, a graduate of Columbia University, and is able to provide an objective, unbiased approach to funds that puts you in a position to get the most out of them.

AMERICAN RESEARCH COUNCIL, LARCHMONT, N.Y.
Distributed to the Trade by The Citadel Press

Investing for Financially Successful Retirement

How This Book Can Help You:

There are many ways individuals build up funds for future retirement — through social security, bank savings, insurance, company profit sharing and pension plans, etc. Investing in stocks, while keeping in mind the goal of financially successful retirement, can be one of the most rewarding ways of putting extra funds to work to provide far more than a minimum fixed income during retirement years.

Now a leading investment analyst shows how to use stocks and bonds to protect your capital against inflation, to make it grow faster and return larger income. He shows you how to set up a plan for your own age and needs and how to invest to attain your goals; you see how to pick stocks for present and future income; what types of stocks including preferreds, give maximum safety; how to use bonds and convertibles in your plan; how to plan for greatest growth of capital; how to use mutual funds and investment companies; how to build tax-free income if you are in high tax brackets, and more.

Sam Shulsky is a noted financial writer and columnist, author of STOCK BUYING GUIDE (150,000 copies sold) and OPPORTUNITIES IN FINANCE. He has written articles for the STOCK EXCHANGE MAGAZINE, READER'S DIGEST, CORONET, NATION'S BUSINESS, etc., writes an investment column syndicated in many newspapers, lectures extensively on financial matters and is presently **Assistant Financial Editor of the New York** Journal American.

See last page for other titles in the Library

AMERICAN RESEARCH COUNCIL, LARCHMONT, N.Y.

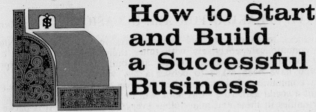

How to Start and Build a Successful Business

How This Book Can Help You:

For millions of individuals, one of the most cherished goals is to set up a successful business of their own. There are indeed many rewards, not just in the possibilities of greatly increased income and financial security, but also in the emotional satisfactions that come from independence and building something of one's own can that be passed along to one's children.

Along with the rewards, however, there are many increased responsibilities and financial risks. But the path can be greatly smoothed by the right knowledge and experience, such as is presented in convenient, practical form in this book. The famed J. K. Lasser Tax Institute has brought together here an extremely useful collection of tested ideas, techniques and methods for assuring business success, increasing profits and avoiding the pitfalls that cause business failures. Here you have at your finger-tips guidance on such topics as—

- Choosing the best form of business—proprietorship, partnership or corporation.
- How to obtain financing and credit.
- What records should be kept for best control and protection.
- Tax-wise savings in business.
- When you want to buy an established business.
- How to organize for profitable expansion.
- Obtaining the best insurance for your business.
- How to handle credit to increase sales volume.
- Protecting your business against theft and fraud.

The J. K. LASSER TAX INSTITUTE is the country's foremost authority on profitable tax and business methods. Author of the bestselling. "Your Income Tax," "How To Save Estate and Gift Taxes" and many other guides for businessmen and other individuals, the Institute has brought together in this book practical help for every individual now in or planning his own business.

AMERICAN RESEARCH COUNCIL, LARCHMONT, N.Y.

EFFECTIVE SPEAKING FOR ALL OCCASIONS   Borden

In business, in community and public affairs, in your social life, the ability to communicate effectively with other individuals can be one of your most useful tools to achieve success and build fruitful relationships. Whether you have been asked to deliver a few words to a group or to serve as a community chairman, invited to meet a prospective employer or to attend a social gathering—this book will help you meet the challenges and opportunities in these and many other everyday situations. It is packed with practical tips on a great variety of topics, such as: Your Platform Manner, Getting Your Message Across, Improving Your Vocabulary, Prior Planning, Think Your Way to Success, People Can Be Fun, Developing Your Personality, Special Advice for Women, the Unseen Audience, Rules of Order and How to Conduct a Meeting, and much more. This book is an invaluable companion and aid to achieving your aims in business, social life and community activity.

ACCOUNTING FOR EVERYDAY PROFIT
by The J. K. Lasser Institute

Here at last in concise, quickly understandable form is the basic "language of business" to help you increase profits, advance more rapidly and establish your financial security. The J. K. Lasser Institute brings you in this book a common sense mastery of accounting principles and practice. Not only does it show you what accounting statements reveal and how they can guide you to the most profitable action, but it also demonstrates how to carry out the accounting procedures that are so important. You actually see all the forms and records, how they are kept, how they are used and what they mean for your own profit and advancement. You will find, too, Different Ways of Doing Business; Applications of Accounting to Better Understanding of Company Reports and Your Investments; Effective Budgeting for Every Purpose; and Profitable Tax Planning that Adds to Your Income. This book will enable you to get ahead faster in your own or any business and it will help you to achieve greater financial security for yourself and your family by a more efficient handling of your own finances, investments and taxes.

You are invited to send for the books you want to read.